The Weary Prophet

PROVIDING PRACTICAL STEPS FOR RESTORATION

Kimberly Moses

Kimberly Moses/Rejoice Essential Publishing

PO BOX 512

Effingham, SC 29541

www.republishing.org

The Weary Prophet/ Kimberly Moses

ISBN-13 978-1-952312-45-8
Library of Congress Control Number: 2020948990

Dedication

THIS BOOK WOULDN'T BE possible without the inspiration of the Holy Spirit. During the Covid-19 pandemic, the Lord constantly downloaded new ideas and opened new opportunities. This book is the fruit of my fellowship with the Lord.

2 Timothy 3:16-17 says, "All scripture is given by inspiration of God, and is profitable for doctrine, for reproof, for correction, for instruction in righteousness: That the man of God may be perfect, thoroughly furnished unto all good works."

Contents

Acknowledgments

I WANT TO THANK ALL the members of my YouTube membership. You guys supported and believed in me when the Lord opened up a new avenue to create new content. You guys are awesome.

I want to thank all my ministry partners, supporters, mentees, spiritual daughters and sons. Thank you for all the prayers and support.

I want to thank my husband for allowing me to write and go forth in my calling.

I want to thank my parents, siblings, family, leaders, and those who encouraged me throughout this journey.

Introduction

MANY PROPHETS HAVE GOTTEN weary as they wait for the promises of God. They have taken their eyes off Jesus and put their eyes on their circumstances instead. There were times that I wanted something so bad that I was anxious. The Bible warns us not to be anxious about anything (Philippians 4:6). I realized that I had some idols in my heart, and I wanted certain things more than I wanted God. I repented and when I stopped idolizing the ideas, then God blessed me with exactly what I wanted in His timing. He had to make sure that I was able to handle what I was asking for. If we aren't careful, then we can turn our backs on God when we get the promise.

Galatians 6:9 says, "And let us not be weary in well doing: for in due season we shall reap if we faint not."

The Greek word for weary (G1573) is '*ekkakeo*' which means to be utterly spiritless or exhausted[1]. How many prophets are exhausted because they aren't spending enough time

1."G1573 - ekkakeō - Strong's Greek Lexicon (KJV)." Blue Letter Bible. Accessed 18 Oct, 2020.

with God? Also, the Strong's definition of 'ekkakeo' means to be weak or faint.

How many times have you felt like you didn't have the strength to go on? Have you wanted to quit and go into the cave? I felt like that many times, but the Holy Spirit wouldn't allow me, so I will not allow you to either. With the same comfort that I received, I am giving it to you.

> *2 Corinthians 1:3-5 says, "Blessed be God, even the Father of our Lord Jesus Christ, the Father of mercies, and the God of all comfort; Who comforteth us in all our tribulation, that we may be able to comfort them which are in any trouble, by the comfort wherewith we ourselves are comforted of God. For as the sufferings of Christ abound in us, so our consolation also aboundeth by Christ."*

We all have to go through our process and sometimes it doesn't happen as soon as we want. Your promises are coming. The prophecy will be fulfilled. Your harvest is nearer than ever. You are about to reap. Just lean on God's strength instead of your own. Many people see prophets as superheroes and put us on pedestals. They don't see the pain, rejection, warfare, and the sacrifices that we make. The Lord gave me this book one day in the shower. He wants to encourage those who have lost hope and feel forgotten. You aren't forgotten because you are on the mind of God. He will never leave us nor forsake us (Deuteronomy 31:6). You are the apple of His eye (Psalms 17:8).

I've been a weary prophet but learned to get a handle on my emotions. In 2014, the Lord had me to write "*Overcoming Emo-*

tions with Prayers," and I felt like I experienced every emotion in that book. I had to go through that so I can write the perfect prayers for someone to get their breakthrough and deliverance. For three years, I had a wilderness season in Colorado Springs that continued when I relocated to South Carolina for a couple of years after that. I experienced warfare that was out of this world and that keeps me praying to God continually. I will further testify throughout this book as we delve into some essential areas that must be cultivated in a prophet's life. Next, I waited to be ordained and connect to the right ministry. In God's timing, that took place and it was well worth the wait. When God blesses, He does it BIG! I often say, "God, I'm 'over encouraged! I wasn't expecting you to go all out but thank you. You are truly good." Get ready because you are about to say the same words. I'm still waiting on many promises, but I trust God's timing and you will learn too as well.

You probably think that a weary prophet isn't biblical. Two examples are John the Baptist and Jeremiah. We will delve deeper into more examples as we go further along. First, John the Baptist became weary when he was in prison for calling out King Herod's sin (Matthew 14:3). He then began to doubt Jesus. He told his disciples to ask Jesus was he the one that the scriptures talk about or should they expect someone else (Matthew 11:3). Let's pause for a moment and think about what just happened. John the Baptist questioned who Jesus was, but the Spirit of God confirmed that Jesus was the one to come when he saw the Holy Spirit ascending upon him like a dove. Also, God spoke out of the cloud, "This is my beloved Son."

Luke 3:22 (NKJV) says, "And the Holy Spirit descended in bodily form like a dove upon Him, and a voice came from heaven which said, "You are My beloved Son; in You I am well pleased."

John the Baptist was able to see the Holy Spirit in the Spirit and hear the voice of God when he wasn't emotionally or feeling weary. Yet, when the battle fatigue set in, he allowed weariness to cloud his judgment and forgot what he witnessed before imprisonment. Have you ever wavered in your faith because of your circumstances?

The next example is Jeremiah. He was known as the weeping prophet because he authored the Book of Lamentations. He often cried over the sins of the people and he wanted to give up (Jeremiah 8:18-12:13; 4:19-6:14).

He witnessed many shifts in leadership: Josiah, Jehoahaz, Jehoiachin, Jehoiakim, King Nebuchadnezzar, Zedekiah, and Pharaoh Neco ll (Jeremiah 1:2-3;46). God appointed him to be a mouthpiece during the calamitous times of battles to point people back to serving the Lord. However, the people ran further away from God and worshipped their idols (Jeremiah 1:15-16). It seemed like the more Jeremiah spoke, the less the people listened (Jeremiah 7:24,27). Their sins infuriated God and broke Jeremiah's spirit. One day, Jeremiah became so weary that he said, "Enough is enough. I will not speak anymore in His name (Jeremiah 20:9)." However, God in His mercy knew exactly what Jeremiah needed. He sent his fire to refresh and replenish the weary prophet. Suddenly, Jeremiah exclaimed, "His fire was shut up in my bones." When you get weary, you want to quit and shrink back into a spiritual cave while forgetting why God appointed you in the first place. Also, when you get weary, you speak irrationally. Don't let weariness be your downfall.

Over the next month, read a devotional daily and meditate on the daily Scripture. Afterward, pray the declarations out loud. You will find supernatural strength and draw closer to the Lord. He has a need for you and you are alive for such a time as this. Shake off the discouragement and let's move forward!

1

Intimacy with the Lord

MANY TIMES, WE CAN get so busy with ministry or working for the Lord that we neglect spending time with Him. I had to realize that doing ministerial work isn't the same as spending quality time with Him. There is a big difference. Many prophets are about to burn out and operating on fumes. Daily we need a fresh anointing. That's why getting in God's presence is vital. In the presence of the Lord is the fullness of joy (Psalm 16:11). I can always tell when someone isn't spending time with God because they are rude, cranky, and have a nasty attitude. How can you say that you have spent time with God when you don't display His love for others? When you spend time with Him, then you will begin to take on His attributes.

Also, spending time with God is an opportunity for you to get refreshed. I pray for so many people every day and it can get tiresome. However, after I get before the Lord, His fire comes upon me and I soak it up. I get my second wind to tackle another day. I get refreshing ideas and the strength that I need to carry on. Sometimes I get secrets from spending time with Him. The Lord shows me things that are to take place in the next season. It's an honor for Him to trust me. He wants to do the same with you.

> *Psalm 25:14 says, "The secret of the LORD is with them that fear him; and he will shew them his covenant."*

One day, I was going through all the routines of doing ministry and I wasn't as intimate with the Lord as I could've been. I disobeyed God because He asked me to do something that was outside of my comfort zone. I went to pray, and I heard the Holy Spirit give me a Bible verse. I turned to the verse and my eyes widened. "What!" What I read wasn't good and I rebuked it because it said that I had a lying spirit. I got so scared and repented for speaking things out of my flesh. I cried out for deliverance and the Lord set me free. From that moment, I vowed to never neglect my time with Him again. I learned to only speak what the Lord tells me and not try to tickle itching ears. Many prophets are speaking things that come from their emotions, flesh, or repeating what they heard. Be careful because you want to make sure that your motives are pure. We don't prophesy for money or to take advantage of someone. We are the Lord's prophets and we don't belong to ourselves.

BENEFITS

1. Joy

In God's presence is the fullness of joy. Whenever I am feeling weary or discouraged, I get into His presence. I may enter into the Holy of Holies weak. But when I leave, I am strengthened. One day, I was heavy because of some warfare that I faced in relationships in ministry. I fell on my face and prayed. A few minutes into the prayer, my eyes opened in the spirit. I saw angels on clouds playing harps and trumpets. Then suddenly, I feel the joy of the Lord deep down into my belly and out of my mouth erupted this continual laughter for about 20 minutes. I couldn't stop. It was like I was at a comedy show. In between laughs, I managed to say, "Lord, stop! I don't want my husband to hear me!" Then I busted out in laughter all over again. The Holy Spirit knew exactly what I needed to get me through the next season, where I faced betrayal and disappointments. His joy kept me going, so I would not give up. I was able to laugh at the devil's attacks through the Holy Spirit. I had received impartation straight from heaven that was contagious. Afterward, many people on my prayer line would burst out laughing as I ministered.

2. Strength

Psalm 29:11 says, "The LORD will give strength to His people; The LORD will bless His people with peace."

The Lord is our refuge. Whenever you are under attack, then go spend time with God. He will give you supernatural strength to continue the task before you. I wanted to quit my prayer ministry so many times. Prophetic intercession is a job where a lot of virtue is released and on the prayer line, prophecy, healing, and deliverance is a daily occurrence. However, the Lord would not allow me to quit. He sent faithful intercessors alongside me to hold up my arms. He placed it on their hearts to honor me and show their appreciation for the work that I was doing. When I decided in my heart to end my prayer line after praying for two years, the Lord put me on center stage at one of my conferences and had women that I had poured into for years to cry their hearts out to me. They told me how much of an impact that I made on them and blessed God for my ministry. When they spoke these words, I repented for my selfishness and the Lord strengthened me at that moment. I thought, "Lord, I had no idea that the ministry meant so much to so many people." The Lord was so gracious to encourage me. Whenever I want to quit, I think about that day. Get out of your feelings, prophet! When we are in our feelings, we can't see correctly. When Jonah got in his feelings, He couldn't see the spiritual awakening taking place among the Ninevites when they repented (Jonah 4:1). The ministry that God has given you is significant. Stop looking at the numbers or the amount of people who support you. Be obedient to God. He will give you strength as He did with me.

3. Secrets

Jeremiah 33:3 says, "Call unto me, and I will answer thee, and show thee great and mighty things, which thou knowest not."

Whenever we spend time with God and work on our intimacy with Him, then He will begin to release secrets. I always compare our relationship with the Lord to a marriage. If our spouse doesn't communicate with us, then we will feel rejected and get upset. Yet, we do that to God. Why would God tell a stranger His secrets? God called Abraham a friend. Even when He wanted to destroy Sodom and Gomorrah, He hesitated until He told Abraham (Genesis 18:17). There were times when I was just praying and lying prostrate before God. Then He spoke things to me that weren't on my mind. He told me who was getting ready to die, what will happen with the school system and the economy. I wrote down what I heard and two weeks later, the prophecy came to pass. These experiences have occurred on numerous occasions. Let's be a friend to God so He can show us great and mighty things.

4. Protection

Psalm 91:1 says, "He that dwelleth in the secret place of the most High shall abide under the shadow of the Almighty."

When we get into the presence of God, He will protect us. His Glory will be our rear guard. The enemy will flee in the glory of God (Isaiah 58:8). When I go through warfare, I rebuke it immediately. Then I get into the presence of the Lord. I worship, praise, and pray. Much prayer equals much power. As I stay hidden underneath his wings and stay close in His shadow, the devil can't touch me. He may try but no weapon formed against me can prosper. Learn how to get in the presence of God and He will not allow any hairs on your head to be harmed.

> *Isaiah 54:17 says, "No weapon that is formed against thee shall prosper; and every tongue that shall rise against thee in judgment thou shalt condemn. This is the heritage of the servants of the Lord, and their righteousness is of me, saith the Lord."*

5. Accuracy

> *John 10:27 says, "My sheep hear my voice, and I know them, and they follow me."*

You have to spend time with God to know His voice. The more time that you spend with God, the level of prophetic accuracy will increase. When I established a prayer altar in my home where the presence of the Lord comes to seek me at the same time daily, then I become more accurate in my gift. The goal wasn't to use God for information and share everything that I heard with others. The goal was to just love and worship the Lord and seek Him without any motives attached. We have to have a hunger for Him and learn how to enjoy time with Him. Every season is different because some seasons it may be more challenging to enter into fellowship than others. However, you have to learn how to press your way through. When

I spend lots of time with God, then I start having nighttime visions and when I prophesy, there is a greater level of detail.

6. Power

1 Corinthians 4:20 says, "For the kingdom of God is not in word, but in power."

You will increase in your spiritual gifts and demonstrate the Kingdom of God when you spend time with Him. The Lord will impart to you and when a demand arises, He will put the gifts on your life in demand. I noticed that when I prayed more and sought the Lord often, then His power flowed through me as never before. He anointed me to cast out devils and to heal the sick. God doesn't want us to just talk about it but be able to demonstrate His glory and power on earth. The same Glory that comes into your prayer closet will manifest publicly when you minister. What you do privately, God will reward you openly. Sometimes, the Lord requires me to shut in and fast for a day or two. When this time is over, then the power of God manifests when I do what He has anointed me to do.

7. Wisdom

Jeremiah 23:18 says, "For who hath stood in the counsel of the LORD, and hath perceived and heard his word? who hath marked his word, and heard it?"

Intimacy with the Lord ensures that we take part in His counsel. Many times, I came to God with so many problems.

After I finished talking, I stilled my spirit and listened. I then heard divine wisdom and instructions. The Lord solved my problems and after prayer, I knew exactly what I had to do. God is concerned with all areas of our lives. He wants us to succeed and delights in our prosperity.

> *Psalm 35:27 says, "Let them shout for joy, and be glad, that favour my righteous cause: yea, let them say continually, Let the Lord be magnified, which hath pleasure in the prosperity of his servant."*

8. Purity

> *Psalm 51:7 says, "Purge me with hyssop, and I shall be clean: wash me, and I shall be whiter than snow."*

As we get before the Lord, He can purify us. His spirit will convict us as necessary to transform us more into the image of His Son Jesus Christ. There were times that I went to God upset and wanted to complain about someone else. The Lord provided me comfort. Then He began to deal with me. He would reveal the bitterness, unforgiveness, jealousy, or the insecurity that I was holding onto. I never forgot when I was frustrated because this lady kept copying off of me. I went to God about her and He said, "What about the times where you copied someone?" His words cut me, but I needed to hear it. We have to keep our eyes on Jesus and count it an honor when people are inspired by the work that we are doing for Him. It's a blessing to motivate and encourage others to walk in their destiny when they see all the things that the Lord is doing through you. I had to surrender and allow Him to purge me and set me free. We have to ask God daily to create in us a pure heart and wash us with hyssop and the blood of Jesus.

> *Psalm 51:10 says, "Create in me a clean heart, O God; and renew a right spirit within me."*

2

Why The Devil Hates Prophets

WARFARE COMES WITH THE calling. Prophets go through persecution, rejection, loneliness, and misunderstanding.

Luke 11:49 (BSB) says, "Because of this, the Wisdom of God said, 'I will send them prophets and apostles; some of them they will kill and others they will persecute."

Prophets might get attacked by the spirit of Jezebel. According to the Blue Letter Bible, the name Jezebel means Baal exalts[2]. Interestingly, Jezebel promoted Baal and Asherah worship in her day. She became very upset when Elijah killed all her prophets, who worshipped those gods (1 Kings 18).

When this spirit attacks prophets, they will forfeit their ministry or assignment. They will allow the person who is operating in that spirit to control them. Lastly, they could die pre-

2. "H348 - 'Iyzebel - Strong's Hebrew Lexicon (KJV)." Blue Letter Bible. Accessed 18 Oct, 2020. https://www.blueletterbible.org//lang/lexicon/lexicon.cfm?Strongs=H348&t=KJV

maturely. Jezebel hated the true prophets of God. She killed them every chance that she had and she threatened to do the same to Elijah (1 Kings 19:2-3).

1 Kings 18:4 says, "... had slaughtered the prophets of the LORD."

Let's look at Jehu's prophecy. He was the man God chose to bring Jezebel down. In this prophecy, you can see that Jezebel killed a lot of prophets.

2 Kings 9:7 (NASB) says, "You shall strike the house of Ahab your master, that I may avenge the blood of My servants, the prophets, and the blood of all the servants of the LORD, at the hand of Jezebel."

You will encounter demonic attacks ever so often. I'm often amazed at how witches find me on social media. I have crossed paths with several of Satan's agents. Sometimes they try to astral project in my bedroom or speak word curses. However, they fail to realize they can't curse what God has blessed (Numbers 23:8). When I say a witch, I am not calling someone a name that I disagree with because several people do. Also, I don't call someone that because I don't like them. I had to correct many people that were underneath my ministry before when they got upset at someone and the first thing that accused that person of being is a witch. I would kindly correct them and say, "Now, you know that lady isn't a witch just because she disagrees with you." Some people humbled themselves when I corrected them while some got offended and cut me off because they couldn't handle my reproof. When I use the term witch, I'm actually referring to who they are in the spirit.

One day, I was talking to my apostle and I was going through some warfare. I kept feeling knives stabbing me in the spirit and I reached out to him for prayer. I said, "I just don't understand why these witches keep finding me." He said, "The prophet is like a light that attracts everything in the spirit." His wise counsel brought clarity and I knew that warfare was just something that prophets have to go through. I will never forget the first time that I felt knives or something sharp stabbing me in the spirit. I was walking through my apartment and I yelled ouch! I felt something stab me hard and then it kept sticking me in different parts of my body. I cried out to the Lord. "God, what is this?" I then heard Him say, "That's witchcraft!" Immediately, I went into prayer and rebuked it. I put on the full armor of God that is listed in Ephesians 6:10-18 and I pleaded the blood of Jesus against the enemy. These prayers were effective and canceled the devil's plans concerning me because of the effectual fervent prayers of the righteous availeth much (James 5:16). Afterward, the stabbing sensation stopped.

When God called me as a prophet, I wasn't knowledgeable at first. I said, "God, I am not a prophet because I'm not an obese Caucasian man with a beard." Later, I had to repent for my lack of ignorance. Once I delved into the Bible and discovered women prophets, I told the Lord, "Yes. I will go all the way with You and not hold back." I had to learn how to embrace my calling over time because sometimes the warfare was intense. I just thought that I could go around prophesying to people, set them free by the power of God then go on my merry way. That wasn't always the case because I encountered a spirit called backlash and retaliation. I had no idea why I got attacked in the spirit after I would pray for someone.

I remember one day, I prayed for this man and the Lord showed me what he enjoyed doing. He loved to go hiking in the mountains. My eyes were opened in the spirit. I began to describe the scenery of the beautiful field of flowers near a bridge crossing over a pond. He knew exactly what I was describing and he told me the name of the location. Next, the Lord filled my mouth with prophecy and I began to prophesy that his wife was going to come back to him. His wife was having an affair and living with another man. When those words came out of my mouth, the spirit of heaviness left him and the peace of God came upon him. The prophecy broke the demonic shackles off his life and he received hope. His marriage got restored about three years after that prophecy. However, after I prayed for him, I started feeling heavy and depressed. It was as if those spirits that broke off the man's life came upon me. Now, I have learned how to pray and bind up those spirits in advance from attacking me.

No matter how powerfully you move in the things of God, the devil hates it. He doesn't want people to be set free and receive the gift of eternal life (Romans 6:23). There are nine main reasons why the devil hates prophets.

1. **Speak the Word of Lord**

Luke 1:70 (NASB) says, "As He spoke by the mouth of His holy prophets from of old."

The devil hates prophets because they speak the word of the Lord. The enemy's job is to kill, steal, and destroy. He doesn't want people to receive hope to hold on to God's promises. Imagine how blessed you are when you receive a prophecy during a trial. During adverse circumstances, you may feel discouraged, your faith may be wavering, and lack optimism. When this happens, you are right where the devil wants you because he loves to kick us when we are down. He is vicious and conniving. When a prophet speaks and tells someone what great things the Lord has in store for them, then all the discouragement leaves. They then get hope to fight for the promises.

When I was in Colorado Springs, I was chronically depressed. I was going through a divorce and felt like my life was over. I just wanted to die because I battled suicidal thoughts. The enemy played on my mind and sometimes I could hear him say, "Why don't you just kill yourself. You are worthless." However, God intervened. He sent prophets to speak into my life to encourage and build me up in the faith. It was supernatural. I would get a random message on social media from a stranger or someone would call me out on their LIVE broadcast and prophesy over me. The prophets spoke over my destiny and revealed the plans that God had in store for me. When the trials intensified, I thought about the prophecies. They gave me the strength that I needed to fight the good fight of faith, which was the last thing the devil wanted. He tried to persuade me to kill myself, but the word of the Lord prevailed.

2. Promote Holiness While Shunning Evil

2 Corinthians 4:4 (ESV) says, "In their case the god of this world has blinded the minds of the unbelievers, to keep them from seeing the light of the gospel of the glory of Christ, who is the image of God."

Satan is the god of this world and he has blinded people's eyes who don't believe in Jesus to the truth of God's Word. The devil wants them to miss out on their opportunity to receive the gift of eternal life that only happens when we accept Jesus in our hearts and live uprightly before the Lord (John 3:16). Jesus promoted holiness and the religious leaders had him crucified. John the Baptist told the King that he was in sin. He was arrested and eventually lost his head (Matthew 14:3,8). Jeremiah was thrown into a cistern/well (Jeremiah 38) and then his head was put in stocks (Jeremiah 20:2). The enemy was influencing people to harm the prophets and try to kill them.

I have been persecuted for righteousness sake. When this occurs, then you know that you are blessed. Jesus told his disciples that they were blessed when they went through persecution because of Him.

Matthew 5:11 says, "Blessed are you when they revile and persecute you, and say all kinds of evil against you falsely for My sake."

I had death threats before and the enemy sent people to try to harm me physically, but God protected me. A true prophet of God will tell people that they need to repent and get back in right standing with God. They will often remind people to be holy as God is holy (1 Peter 1:16). The enemy hates God's prophets because they are a threat to his kingdom. Their words of corrections are constantly in people's ears to return to their first love, who is Jesus Christ.

3. They Expose

Luke 8:17 (NKJV) says, "For nothing is secret that will not be revealed, nor anything hidden that will not be known and come to light."

Prophets function in the revelatory gifts of the Holy Spirit, which are the word of wisdom, word of knowledge, or gifts of discerning of spirits. These gifts will expose the plans of the enemy and once the schemes of hell are revealed, we can pray against it. God will show His prophet the destruction that lays waste at noonday (Psalm 91:6). God will reveal the plans of the enemy that are spoken in private. Elisha was able to pick up the conversation that his enemy (King of Syria) spoke in his bedchamber. Once he got the information, he, then, warned others so they would be spared from an attack (2 Kings 6). The King of Syria got so upset that he sent an army after Elisha, but no weapon formed God's prophets will prosper.

Many times, I prayed for someone and the Lord showed me the hidden things in their heart such as sexual sin, bitterness, unforgiveness, or pride. Once it was brought to the surface and dealt with through repentance and deliverance, the person received the healing they desired from any physical infirmities. Also, the Lord will wake me up in the middle of the night and allow me to intercede for someone. The Lord will give me assignments to warn people about upcoming attacks from the enemy so they can be discerning and walk circumspectly.

Ephesians 5:15-17 says, "See then that ye walk circumspectly, not as fools, but as wise, redeeming the time, because the days are evil. Wherefore be ye not unwise, but understanding what the will of the Lord is."

4. Imparting While Equipping

Prophets are called to impart the anointing that they carry into others, which is part of the prophet's reward. Matthew 10:41 says, "He who receives a prophet in the name of a prophet shall receive a prophet's reward."

You will be rewarded with whatever gift or anointing on the prophet's life that you honor. When a prophet imparts a greater level of anointing that you may lack, then you will be propelled into your destiny and walk in a deeper dimension of the Glory. Jesus gave gifts to the body of Christ (the five-fold ministry), so they can equip the believers to do the work of the ministry.

Ephesians 4:8, 11-12 (ESV)
Therefore it says, "When he ascended on high he led a host of captives, and he gave gifts to men." And he gave the apos-

tles, the prophets, the evangelists, the shepherds, and teachers, to equip the saints for the work of ministry, for building up the body of Christ,

Prophets may be called to train up others and equip them to walk in the purpose that God has for them. The enemy doesn't want believers to know who they are in Christ because then they will become the ultimate threat to the kingdom of darkness. When a person is equipped, they will be just as Jesus was who came to destroy the works of darkness.

1 John 3:8 says, "For this purpose the Son of God was manifested, that he might destroy the works of the devil."

God has used me to birth people in their ministries. He also has used me to impart spiritual gifts to people.

5. A Supernatural Release

Prophets have anointings to break up fallow ground or the hard places in our lives. Once this occurs, a harvest can take place. We can grow in the things of God, mature, and produce fruits. Here are two examples of God's prophets (Hosea and Jeremiah) speaking similar messages:

Hosea 10:12 says, "Sow to yourselves in righteousness, reap in mercy; break up your fallow ground: for it is time to seek the LORD, till he come and rain righteousness upon you."

Jeremiah 4:3 says, "For thus saith the LORD to the men of Judah and Jerusalem, Break up your fallow ground, and sow not among thorns."

God told Jeremiah when He called him that he was giving him an anointing to root out, pull down, destroy, throw down, build, and plant, which are necessary actions of uprooting demonic strongholds and planting the word of God. In other words, the deliverance anointing on the prophet's life can uproot some deep-rooted issues of the soul. The soulish realm (the flesh) is where the devil attacks (Galatians 5:16-26).

Jeremiah 1:10 says, "See, I have this day set thee over the nations and over the kingdoms, to root out, and to pull down, and to destroy, and to throw down, to build, and to plant."

If you feel stuck by demonic oppression, then a prophet can speak into your life and cause a supernatural release. It will be like a domino effect. Things will start moving forward and it will happen consecutively. Many have testified that when they called my prayer line and receive prayer, then God causes the blessings to flow. The enemy doesn't want us blessed. He would rather have us oppressed by him.

6. Shift The Atmosphere To Cause Momentum

Prophets can carry and shift an atmosphere. When King Saul came into a company of prophets, he prophesied all day and the anointing was so heavy that he came out of his clothes and started to prophesy naked (1 Samuel 19:23). He probably got hot and started sweating because God's presence is like a consuming fire (Hebrews 12:29). There were times when I ministered where I had to take off my suit jacket, blazer, or jacket for the same reason. Saul and his men, who were on the way to kill David met the company of prophets led by Samuel. These prophets created a prophetic atmosphere that made it easy for anyone to prophesy because God's Spirit would come upon them (1 Samuel 19).

I remember at one of my conferences, the atmosphere was full of resistance because an agent of Satan had come to hinder the move of God. When it was time to open up the service, I saw a brick wall before me. I prayed until I saw it crumble. Immediately, I felt a release then started to feel a wave of glory come into the room. I handed the microphone to the worship leader and we entered the presence of the Lord freely. Also, there were times where I opened my mouth then the fire of God came in so strong through the telephone, videos, and even in person. God used me to bring an atmosphere because I had been spending time with him. The devil doesn't want people to be liberated in Jesus Christ. He would rather have people in an oppressive atmosphere, so they don't get their breakthrough. When a prophet shows up, he knows that they carry the power of the Lord to shift the atmosphere.

7. Empower

Prophets have a special gift to empower people to be all they can be in Jesus Christ. Prophecy is to edify, comfort, and exhort (1 Corinthians 14:3). Prophets encourage people to walk in destiny, seek God, pray, fast, worship, tithe, serve, honor, obey God, walk in humility, and so much more. The devil gets nervous when a believer realizes who they are in Christ because they will begin to walk in authority. As a result, God's Kingdom will be manifested on earth through His servants as they are empowered (Romans 8:19-22).

> *Luke 10:19 (NKJV) says, "Behold, I give you the authority to trample on serpents and scorpions, and over all the power of the enemy, and nothing shall by any means hurt you."*

Prophets carry a big responsibility as they encourage people to stay in the will of God. The enemy hates when people are strengthened in their faith because they were once on the broad path, but now they are on the straight and narrow.

> *Matthew 7:13-14 (ESV) "Enter by the narrow gate. For the gate is wide and the way is easy that leads to destruction, and those who enter by it are many. For the gate is narrow and the way is hard that leads to life, and those who find it are few."*

God has used me to empower people to see the gifts and talents inside of them that they aren't able to see themselves. Afterward, they can write their books, launch their business, and step out of their comfort zones.

8. They Loose Prosperity

Prophets can bring prosperity to people's lives. Some may disagree, but when you closely study the lives of various prophets throughout the Bible, you will begin to see it differently. Abraham was a prophet that had so much wealth that his herdsmen and his nephew Lot's herdsmen began to argue. They had accumulated so much wealth that there wasn't enough room for both of them on the same land (Genesis 13:7). Moses was known as a prophet who spoke to God face to face (Exodus 33:11). He had the spirit of wisdom, which generated wealth (Deuteronomy 34:9). It took a lot of resources to make the tabernacle (Exodus 25–31; 35–40). These chapters show that the finest material was used to build something elaborate for the ark of the covenant to rest. Aaron (Moses' prophet) and the children of Israelites must have had wealth as well (Exodus 12:35-37) because they had enough gold to make a golden calf (Exodus 32:21-24). Many people would not give away something as valuable as gold to be molded into a statue. The Israelites were well taken care of in the wilderness. They were prosperous because what was on their leader's life came down into their lives. The anointing flows from the head down or from the beard to the skirt (Psalm 133:2).

2 Chronicles 20:20 says, "Believe in the LORD your God, so shall ye be established; believe his prophets, so shall ye prosper."

Once a pastor pulled me to the side. He was upset because I said that a prophet could bring prosperity into people's lives.

I stood on the above Scripture and I told him that he was free to disagree, but God had told me otherwise. Elisha had a close relationship with God that God spoke to him about the secrets spoken in the King's bedchamber (2 Kings 6:12). One day a widow cried out to the prophet that the bill collector was about to take her two sons. Elisha asked her what she had in her home. She replied that she only had a jar of oil. The prophet instructed her to get jars from her neighbors, empty them, and pour the oil into the jars. The oil kept flowing until she ran out of jars. God brought prosperity into her life and caused an economy to open up. She now had a business where she sold oil, paid her debt, and lived off the rest. Before then, she had no other options to make money. God wants you blessed.

After God called me off my job in the hospital, He gave me ideas to create multiple streams of income in my life. He gave me books to write, trainings, CDs, a magazine, a publishing business, and then a beauty business. Then He opened up doors for me to make money on social media by having a large following. He made sure that I wasn't broke regardless of who sowed into me or not. He didn't want me to depend on others but only depend on Him. He wanted to make sure that I had the right motives so I could just do ministry without having money as the priority. When my motives became right, God placed on people's hearts to bless me without even asking. God had me training and mentoring others to open up supernatural economies in their lives.

I have received multiple testimonies of praying and releasing prophecy into someone's life. Afterwards, the money came that they believed for, they followed the instructions that God gave to open up a stream of income, and the blessing that was held up got released. The devil hates prophets releasing prosperity into people's lives because he knows that if you don't have any money, then you don't have a voice. Your influence will be small. Those with money can reach more people and get the word out about what they are doing. When you have wealth, you will be able to bless more people and do Kingdom things such as feeding the hungry, clothing the poor, and providing resources for the broken. The enemy would love to keep you broke because he knows it's stressful and a distraction to your purpose.

When you don't have money, then you aren't as focused on God's agenda. You are more concerned about where your next meal will come from, and how the bills will get paid? When I was in the wilderness, I was broke initially. It was stressful but I was determined to persevere. I said, "God I will serve you if I am only skin and bones. I will serve you with or without food. I will serve you with or without money." I endured the trials and learned how to use my faith, which was the thing the devil didn't want me to do. Once I learned how to use faith, I learned how to prophesy over the valley of dry bones and see the manifestation of my words. The devil has caused many people into believing that they have to be broke and they have developed a poverty mentality that caused them to lose their effectiveness in their assignment.

9. Revelation

Prophets can often look in the Word of God and see something beyond the Scriptures. For instance, they can look in the Bible and come across the Scripture that says, "The Lord is my shepherd." From there, they begin to get a Rhema word from Heaven that is uplifting. They will break down what a shepherd is and make it relevant to the believer's life and the trials that they are facing. They will begin to expound on this one verse and the Holy Spirit will pull out new things that the prophet never preached before. The Lord has used me in this way several times. Often, I have to record myself when I teach, so I don't lose the revelatory words that the Lord drops in my mouth.

Prophets can get complete sermons just from cooking, walking, and seeing something that stood out to them. Once I saw a video that was made by a Christian comedian. The title was something about how prophets get messages. The comedian was cooking then reached into the cabinet to grab the salt. At that moment, she stopped because she received a word about not losing our saltiness and we are salt of the earth. I laughed so hard at that video because that hit home for me. I could be taking a shower and get a message of encouragement if the body wash leaked everywhere, the tub was clogged, the showerhead broke, the water going on my skin, and the smell of the soap. Sometimes in those moments, I can hear the Holy Spirit speak a word and use my experiences to encourage others. For example, once my husband was using this Old Spice body wash that was dark red. He didn't snap the lid close and it fell over on the shower rack. It dripped down the wall of the shower and it looked like blood. I got a prophetic word at that moment that I was covered in the blood of Jesus and preached a Monday Motivation on that incident. Another time, I saw a face in the clouds and I prophesied based on what the Holy Spirit gave me when I saw it. Have you ever received prophetic messages based on your surroundings?

Prophets sometimes see far ahead and deep into a situation. It's amazing how God will allow a prophet to get a glimpse into the future. The prophets of old or the prophets in the Old Testament prophesied about Jesus' birth centuries before He was born (Isaiah 9:6). Zechariah and Daniel prophesied some of His attributes and what was to come in the end times (Zechariah 9-14; Daniel 10-12). Malachi and Isaiah prophesied about John the Baptist preparing the way for Jesus (Malachi 3:1; Isaiah 40:3). There are great men and women of God that have been called home to glory but prophesied wars, revivals, pandemics, economic crashes, and new technology. An example is David Wilkerson, who prophesied things thirty to forty years ago that are now happening in 2020. Some other generals in eternity with similar prophecies are Oral Roberts and Smith Wigglesworth. God has given me books that were before my time and I wrote them. When they were released, very few saw the vision, but eventually, they caught up and embraced what the Lord gave me. One book I authored with this problem is, "Overcoming Emotions with Prayers." When I wrote it in 2014, I didn't know any ministers talking about emotions or emotional healing. Now it's become more prevalent because the devil attacks believers in that area.

Prophets make great historians. God can open up a prophet's eyes so they can see what occurred in the past. Moses wrote the Pentateuch or the first five books of the Bible. The Lord supernaturally opened his eyes to see the events and the lives of Adam, Eve, Noah, Abraham, and others. Even though stories were passed down to the next generation, there is no way that he could have known various details unless the Lord revealed it.

The devil doesn't want you to get life-changing information because it will shift someone's life. He would rather have you ignorant and stuck on one dimension. Whenever you get a revelation about something, then you start to have access to it. Then you begin to walk in it. For instance, God showed me weapons in the Bible and I wrote a book, "Warfare Strategies: Biblical Weapons." After I received a revelation about these things, then I began to apply it to my prayer life. Afterward, I was able to break through the oppression the enemy tried to place upon me previously. Many have testified that the book broke demonic strongholds and they use the prayers inside regularly. Another example is when the Lord revealed to me about the word of knowledge and how it operated. I had never heard of it before and I started functioning in this gift after the Lord instructed me to do a seven-day fast. Once the realm of supernatural information opened to me, I started walking in it and didn't look back.

In summary, the nine reasons why the devil hates prophets are because they speak the word of the Lord, promote holiness while shunning evil, expose, impart while equipping, provide supernatural release, shift the atmosphere to cause momentum, empower, loose prosperity, and offer revelation.

3

Avoid Pitfalls

WHEN A PROPHET GETS weary, impatience sets in, and if they are not careful, then they can fall into pitfalls or Satanic traps. The enemy traps prophets into sexual sin, greed, idolatry, or divination. I have witnessed various prophets stumble and once they do, it was hard for them to make a comeback. Let's discuss each one.

1. Sexual Sin.

God pronounced judgment upon Jezebel because she seduced his servants to commit sexual immorality and eat foods that were offered to idols (Revelation 2:20). It is rumored that prophets have an intense sexual appetite because they are sensitive to the spirit realm. A prophet that I used to follow on social media was discussing sex and once said, "Whenever he finished ministering, he then needed his wife to minister to him." He wasn't talking about spiritual nourishment in this statement. Our flesh desires sex, but we have to yield those urges unto the Lord. He will strengthen us to live holy lives and not stumble. Many sexual scandals have occurred in the body of

Christ and when this comes out, the minister loses their sphere of influence. They may get restored to the body but never reach the same prominence as they did before they fell. Many ministers have had children by their mistresses and try to cover it up. Some aren't as fortunate because their sin gets blasted everywhere on social media.

The devil is always plotting and scheming. He knows what our flesh desires and what we are attracted to. He will send someone that is pleasing to the eye to seduce you. He wants to ruin your credibility and weaken the authority that you have been giving through Jesus Christ. If you sin and allow the devil into your life, then it will be harder to get rid of him. He won't budge when you pray prayers of deliverance or healing. He will say, "Hey. You opened this portal and allowed me access to your life by this soul tie when you committed sexual sin." When this happens, we must repent, cut off the source of the sin, and get back into alignment with God. We must live holy lives to have a greater dimension of authority over the devil.

When I first got called into the prophetic ministry, I encountered a group of false prophets. They cursed and fornicated. I knew what they were doing was wrong, so I cut that connection off. One day, I became friends with one of them. He gave me a sob sorry that his girlfriend died. He called her a godly woman, but when I looked at her photo, there was no light of the gospel in her only darkness. Her attire wasn't appropriate for someone who was truly godly and they were in fornication when she was alive. One day, the gentlemen called me on skype. We started talking about the prophetic ministry then he shifted the conversation. He said, "God tells me to masturbate." I called him a liar and hung up on him. He kept trying to reach me. When he couldn't he cursed me out on skype then in my text messages. Shortly after that experience, his apostle sent me some books. The title of one book was opening the third eye. The title of the other book had the F word in it. It was something like, "F the bucket." I felt so grieved in my spirit. I had an eerie feeling come upon me as I held the books in my hands. I immediately threw the books into the dumpster.

Another time, I wanted to put this emerging prophet in my Christian magazine, "*Rejoice Essential Magazine.*" However, he gave me the run-around and we never conducted the interview. A few months later, his wife put on social media everything that the prophet was doing. He was traveling and prophesying, but he was committing sexual sin. It was sad to see this young man fall. His wife divorced him as he lost everything and hit rock bottom. The devil had him where he wanted him. It was heartbreaking to see him post on social media, "I'm so depressed. I don't want to live anymore. God help. The pain is so real. It's too much for me to handle." When he sinned against God, the peace that he once had left his life and the enemy had a legal right to torment him. The thief comes to steal, kill, and destroy.

Years ago, there was a popular Christian television show with a husband and wife couple. They were rich and had everything that they could have wanted. However, the fame went to their heads and they grew further away from God. The husband started to mess around with prostitutes behind his wife's back. When the prostitute wanted to come out about what had happened, the husband paid her some hush money. For some reason, the lady didn't want any more money and went to the media and exposed the husband. When this came out, another well-known preacher bashed the husband for his sins and shortly after, he got exposed for sleeping with a prostitute. Both ministries fell and were never the same. Many people got hurt and lost their jobs because these ministries employed a lot of people. The husband and wife team ended up getting a divorce while the husband served time for money laundering. We have to realize that our actions affect more than just us. It's not only about us. So much is at stake.

There were times in my singleness the enemy tried to sneak in and cause me to stumble. I decided to go all the way with God and not mess around. I want to be the real deal and preach what I was living. While I waited for my husband, the enemy sent a few counterfeits. The first man was bold. He saw me on fire for God and knew that if he pretended that he wanted God, then I would let him in. Since I was vulnerable and healing from divorce, I still had wounds that weren't healed. I enjoyed talking to this man daily, praying, and reading the Bible. However, after four months, this man started to play games. He started avoiding my phone calls then he would send me porn. He begged me to have sex with him. I blocked this man and never spoke to him again. I cried because I had wasted time and energy. I had grown to care for this man but he was sent by the devil to derail my destiny. After that experience, I realized that I wasn't in any shape to date. I got lost in my purpose and served God with everything within me. In that process, God healed my heart. I had put boundaries in place so I wouldn't sin against God. I didn't talk on the phone late to men. I didn't allow any men to come to my apartment. I didn't entertain flirty men in my inbox on social media. At the right time, God sent my husband. God can keep you because He did it for me. I told God that I was submitting my sexual desires unto Him so I wouldn't sin against Him even in my mind. You can't ponder on those sexual thoughts. Cast it down immediately. Don't let sexual sin be your downfall.

2. Greed

Many prophets start off right in the sight of God but along the way, they allow greed to set in. Balaam started off on the right path in ministry. He once said that he could only speak what the Lord tells him to speak. Numbers 23:12 (CEV) says, "Balaam answered, "I can say only what the LORD tells me." However, greed set in and he led people astray into sexual sin and caused them to eat foods offered to idols (Numbers 25:16; 31:6,14). As a result of Balaam's sin, he gave people horrible advice and ended up being slew by a sword. Sin equals death (Romans 6:23).

Many prophets realize that they can make a lot of money with the gifts that the Lord has blessed them with. At first, their heart may be in alignment with the Lord. Over time, if they don't do daily heart checks and allow the Lord to purge them, then greed will take its effect. Daily we must pray Psalm 51:10, "Lord, create in me a pure heart." The Bible warns us that we can't serve two masters: God or mammon (money). The choice on who you serve is up to you because the love of money is the root of all evil. No amount of money will ever satisfy a greedy person because they will just want more and do whatever it takes to get it. Often when you prophesy, people will want to bless you because you gave them the word of the Lord. You must use wisdom in this area because many people have stumbled. They began to have the wrong motives and prophesied to people for monetary gain instead of them being transformed in Christ.

Jesus had to pass the test in the wilderness when the tempter came. He took Jesus to the top of the pinnacle and said, "I will give you everything that you see here today if you just bow down and worship me." Jesus stood his ground and used the word. If Christ did it, then so can we because we have the Holy Spirit living inside. The Holy Spirit is our helper. Imagine how many people have failed when the tempter came. They got caught up in what they saw and sold out. They stopped preaching Jesus, holiness, and the Cross. Then they started to preach fleshly messages that provoked emotions to get people to dig deep into their pockets. You can't look at people like a dollar sign or a way to be fed. You have to view people as souls and Christ's sheep. We will have to give an account one day if our motives aren't pure. God will sometimes allow people who are big tithers to stop giving to you so He can test what's in your heart. Once you prove that your motives are pure, then He can trust you to lead His people.

When a person wants to bless you with outrageous gifts or buy you things for the wrong reason, then turn it down. True prophets of God don't prophesy for money only psychics do. People have stumbled because they allowed people to buy them a house and car in exchange for prophecy. We prophesy for free and if God places it on someone's heart to bless us, then that's between Him and the individual. Many scandals have occurred in the body of Christ where preachers acted like they had the gifts of the word of knowledge. The preachers would look on contact cards that a person filled out, their social media pages, or the internet. They would gather information about an individual and while they were preaching, they called the person's name, address, or some other information they found. The person is not aware where the minister got the information from and they feel that it was God. However, it wasn't. Once the minister tells them their name and birthday, they then give a generic prophecy. The person receiving ministry is so overwhelmed they then begin to give large sums of money. They think, "Surely, this must be God because the preacher knew my birthday." Many scams have been exposed.

Perhaps the minister did have a gift, but due to greed, the Holy Spirit stopped speaking to them, and desperation set in that led them to deceive people. There were times when I had no money in my account and a person found me on social media. They looked up my information and contacted me by email. The email read like this: "Hello. I will give you $800 if you call me and prophesy to me." Again, psychics get on the phone and allow people to pay them for their predictions. At that moment, I had to resist the enemy and submit to God. I refused that offer and trusted God to provide for me. I realized that the enemy comes when you are weak or have a need trying to get you to stumble. Since I did the right thing, God always made sure that I was taken care of financially.

We must not sell out and we can't be brought by people. If that is the case, then they can control what we do. Then what we can preach or prophesy will be limited. Many preachers won't preach on sin because someone invited them to speak at their event and said, "Hey. I will give you ten thousand dollars if you don't preach about homosexuality." The minister agreed. What happens if God sent that person there to speak about that topic, but they allowed greed to hinder what the Holy Spirit wanted to do in the service. Remember, we have already been brought with a price by the blood of Jesus (1 Corinthians 6:20).

When I was new in my calling as a prophet, a lot of people wanted to mentor me. One prophet kept gravitating towards me, but his motives weren't pure. His messages were always about money and he lived a questionable lifestyle. He was a practicing homosexual in high school and it was rumored that he was on the down-low with other ministers. He married a woman as a cover-up, but he wasn't invested in the marriage. He called me a few times to give me advice on ways to make money. The ideas were great, but not right for me. In return, I would counsel him to fight for his marriage because God hates divorce. My spirit couldn't connect with his so I had to put some distance between us. He once told a mutual friend, "I don't care about those N....I just want their money." When I heard those words, I was hurt because he was in ministry for the wrong reasons. We have to love God and love His people (Matthew 22:37-39). This prophet ended up going through public humiliation for his conniving ways. Eventually, I cut ties with this individual because bad company corrupts good morals. If we hang out with people with bad habits, we will pick up those bad traits (1 Corinthians 15:33).

3. Idolatry

Prophets must not get caught up in idolatry or the worship of idols. The prophet may not practice idolatry, but they might become an idol in someone's life. Whatever you put before God, it becomes an idol. The prophetic ministry is a blessing and prophets move in power. When people see the signs, wonders, and miracles, they may begin to put the minister on a pedestal. They will view them as a god. Some people want to worship prophets instead of God. Prophets have to always give God the glory instead of taking it for themselves. When this occurs, we must always point people back to Jesus.

Isaiah 42:8 (ESV) says, "I am the LORD; that is my name; my glory I give to no other, nor my praise to carved idols."

God has used me in the miraculous realm where limbs grew out evenly, lumps dissolved, deaf ears open, fractures healed, chronic pain healed, asthma healed, dental miracles, and more. After each miracle, I stop and say, "Let's give God praise for what He has done." I do this purposefully so people can take their eyes off me and place them back on God. I want to make sure that people know that I didn't do the miracle, but the Holy Spirit did. I have met several people who tried to worship me and I had to stop them. They tried to puff up my head and one time, someone bowed down and begged to touch my feet. I tell people that I am flesh just like them. I encourage people that they can move miraculously too and provide training often.

One time, the Lord gave me a word of knowledge while I was in the gas station. I was tired and had a headache. I just picked up my kids from school and I just wanted to go home and put dinner on. Suddenly while I was paying for the gas inside the store, my legs started hurting. I looked up and coming into the store was a man who was limping. I felt his pain, so I waited while he brought his beef and cigarettes. I approached him boldly and told him that God wanted me to pray for him. He agreed and I laid my hands on his shoulder and commanded his healing. Miraculously, the pain left out of his leg and people were starring as they watched what was happening. The man started thanking me for healing him. I said, "Jesus healed you today. Not me. Remember that." Then I walked away. I planted a seed of the gospel into this man's life and probably interrupted his plans to get a buzz from the alcohol and cigarettes.

Sometimes on my prayer line, new people will give me the glory for their healing and immediately, I correct them. However, some prophets don't and the power goes to their head. Some people won't even pray first. They come directly to me. I tell them that I am not Jesus. I urge them to get their own prayer life. I don't mind praying for people but I don't want to handicap anymore by doing all the prayer for them. My prayers can't get them to heaven. They have to have their own relationship with Jesus to get in.

King Nebuchadnezzar wanted people to worship him and bow down at his statue. However, Shadrach, Meshach, and Abednego knew better and refused. As a result, they were thrown in the fire but God saved them (Daniel 3). God will bless you for standing up for righteousness and refusing idolatry.

Some prophets are prideful and caught up in how accurate their gift is while forgetting the source. God never takes the gifts back once they are distributed.

Romans 11:29 (NKJV) says, "For the gifts and the calling of God are irrevocable."

You can do things in His name but not make it into heaven.

Matthew 7:21-23 (NKJV), "Not everyone who says to Me, 'Lord, Lord,' shall enter the kingdom of heaven, but he who does the will of My Father in heaven. Many will say to Me in that day, 'Lord, Lord, have we not prophesied in Your name, cast out demons in Your name, and done many wonders in Your name?' And then I will declare to them, 'I never knew you; depart from Me, you who practice lawlessness!"

All that power is going to their head and they are giving over to a reprobate mind. As a result, they become false teachers of the Bible and become a heretic and start a cult.

Romans 1:28 says, "And even as they did not like to retain God in their knowledge, God gave them over to a reprobate mind, to do those things which are not convenient;"

David Koresh was a cult leader in Waco, Texas. He used his power to lead people astray and to take advantage of children sexually. People that he brainwashed thought he was a god and ended up losing their lives following behind him. I met a minister years ago who has a controversial ministry. I heard rumors about him, but there was no concrete evidence in the accusations. They would say something like, "He's a liar. He got caught lying in court and it's all on social media. He is greedy. Something about him isn't right." It seemed like a bunch of speculation and I know how it feels when people don't like you for no solid reason at all. I decided to give him a chance and went to one of his services that he held in my area. Honestly, I enjoyed it but then over a few weeks, I started to notice that he lacked godly character. He boasted that he was the second Moses and how powerful he was in the spirit. He cursed people with cancer if they tried to leave his ministry. He set himself up as a god and women from around the globe would sleep with him. He didn't take correction for his actions from his peers. He would say that he ranked higher than them and that the people who tried to correct him didn't have any real power. When I was able to prove the facts, I blocked him on social media and never followed anything else he had going on. His ministry is a cult and this minister is the people's god in that organization.

Another example was this young prophet. He is the exact replica of what a 'pretty boy' represents. Looks to him is everything and women who follow his ministry are mesmerized by it. They idolized this prophet and changed their last names to his last name. The prophet has got caught making sex tapes and has been married several times. These women give this prophet all their money and call him, "Jesus in the flesh." The prophet moves in a strong demonic power and has the spirit of seduction. Even some men are caught up in his spell. One day, a lady came to me about him and I told her the truth that he was false. She didn't believe me, so I took her to the Bible and compared it to the sinful actions of this prophet. Immediately, her eyes were opened and she ended up leaving that ministry.

The devil wants people to set themselves up as gods because he knows one day they will receive eternal damnation. He doesn't want people to get the fullness of the truth of the gospel of Jesus Christ. We should never want power more than we want Jesus. People are idolizing power, fame, and riches, which eventually causes their downfall. Sadly, ministries have been cut short due to idolatry. Either the person dies prematurely or gets imprisoned for some crime. Remember, God is a jealous God. Put Him first place in your life and don't become a god in someone's life.

4. Divination

As a prophet, it is easy to get into divination when you feel like you always have to perform and your motives aren't right. Divination is when you get information from a source other than the Holy Spirit. The source could be from another deity, tarot cards, crystals, and other inanimate objects. God warns us not to practice divination.

Deuteronomy 18:10-12 (NKJV) says "There shall not be found among you anyone who makes his son or his daughter pass[through the fire, or one who practices witchcraft (divination), or a soothsayer, or one who interprets omens, or a sorcerer, 11 or one who conjures spells, or a medium, or a spiritist, or one who calls up the dead. 12 For all who do these things are an abomination to the LORD..."

People don't realize that when the devil gives them power, there are strings attached. The portal to hell and the demonic realm is now open in their lives. They start seeing demons and feeling an eerie presence. They no longer feel the peace of God. Some have sold their souls to the devil or made covenants with him for accuracy. Many prophets in Africa and some Caribbean islands are known to have a form of godliness but denying the power thereof. They pretend to represent Jesus Christ but are deep in darkness just to flow in the supernatural.

Some prophets started off right in the sight of God but then got into witchcraft and now are functioning witches or warlocks (males). They use prophecy to control and manipulate people. They curse people when the Bible tells us to bless and not curse.

Romans 12:14 (NKJV) says, "Bless those who persecute you; bless and do not curse."

These prophets feel like they have to always use their gifts to make money. Yet they fail to realize that if God is not speaking, then they need to be quiet. When they stop hearing the Holy Spirit, they get desperate and seek other mediums for information. King Saul got so desperate once to get information. Initially, he kicked the witches out of the land, but when he disobeyed God, the Spirit of the Lord left him. No matter how much he tried to hear from God, he couldn't hear anything. He then disguised himself and sought a witch to bring up Samuel or the dead prophet's spirit. Saul heard that he would die soon after in battle. Once we open up doors to the enemy, he will do what he does best, which is to kill, steal, and destroy everyone in his path.

Some prophets will tell people what they want to hear and tickle their ears with false prophecy (2 Timothy 4:3). Their motives aren't to draw people to Christ or to transform lives. Their motives are to get rich and drain people financially. God doesn't want us to be money hungry. He will sustain us for having pure motives. Many people have sought me and if I didn't hear anything, then I told them that. Some got upset because I didn't prophesy them a husband or wealth. I told them that I could only say what God says. Years ago, a friend told me that she gave this lady apostle ten thousand dollars over time. The apostle was false and did some questionable acts. She told my friend to get some salt and let her pray over it and sprinkle it around her house outside. My friend obeyed, then things got worse in her life. She kept coming back to the apostle and giving more money. My friend's marriage was in shambles and the apostle preyed on it. She would say, "God said give me $200 and your husband will come home in 2 weeks." My friend sowed the money and in two weeks, her husband was nowhere to be found. When my friend came to me and confessed what she was doing, I could tell that she was underneath some spell or mind control. I prayed and it broke off her. She came to her right senses and cut ties with this lady. She struggled for many months as she paid back all that debt. She took out credit cards and loans to give money to the lady.

There is money to be made in divination. We can see this with the girl with the spirit of divination. Her master's made a lot of money from her. Once Apostle Paul and men cast out that spirit, the owners couldn't profit off the girl anymore.

> *Acts 19:19 (NASB) says, And many of those who practiced magic brought their books together and began burning them in the sight of everyone; and they counted up the price of them and found it fifty thousand pieces of silver."*

In the Scripture above, you can see the value of demonic books cost a lot of money. It's crazy! Psychics are paid to be on television and other platforms, but most preachers have to pay to be on these platforms. The world takes care of its own. The world didn't receive Jesus and it won't receive true prophets (John 1:10; 15:18-19; 17:16). We are heavenly citizens, so we are passing through (Hebrews 11:13-16; 1 Peter 2:11; Philippians 3:20).

Once this prophet I used to follow became pressured to perform. He was at the pinnacle of his ministry and when he prophesied about future events, people listened because his gift was so accurate. However, he started to fornicate and commit other sins. As a result, he wasn't hearing from the Lord and he got desperate. He looked up a psychic and repeated all her predictions verbatim. He got exposed when evidence came out and none of the predictions came to pass. This prophet started to operate in divination when he didn't seek God but turned to a psychic instead.

I once did ministry with a woman who had confided in me. She told me that the information from psychics and prophets are the same. She said, "It's all accurate." She later turned into a functioning witch. She got mad at God because her marriage failed. She turned to crystals for healing. She started teaching things that were false such as God was a woman and exalting the universe and astrological myths. She had demonic symbols on her social media networks. It was so sad to see her fall. I prayed for her to get deliverance for weeks. Then one day, the Lord spoke to me, "She made her choice to serve other gods. Stop praying for her."

Another prophet went around prophesying hours daily. His words fell to the ground and didn't come to pass because they came from his flesh and not God's Spirit. He would make up things just to get people to sow into him. Guard your heart because out of it comes the issues of life. Don't let the need for money, power, and fame be your downfall. If you seek God first and His righteousness, then everything will be added to you. It's best to wait on the Lord and get full of His word so you can resist the tempter when he comes. Walk in the spirit, so you don't fulfill the lust of your flesh.

4

Mind

Hebrews 12:3 says, "For consider him that endured such contradiction of sinners against himself, lest ye be wearied and faint in your minds."

THE ENEMY LOVES TO attack prophets in their mind. His goal is to cause you to forget about the sacrifice that Jesus endured for humanity while placing your thoughts on everything that is going wrong in your life. The Scripture above warns us that we can grow weary, faint in our minds, weak in our souls, or lose heart when we take our focus off Jesus and the purpose of our assignment. When a prophet gets weary, their mind can play tricks on them. They will find themselves thinking on thoughts contrary to the Word of God such as, "My prayers aren't effective. What's the point of praying? I might as well get comfortable because things will never change. It's too hard, so I give up." To make matters worse, the enemy will come up and prey on that weariness and suggest that you should stop what you are doing for God or just walk away from everything. Has this happened to you before? Also, the enemy can cause you to assume something without knowing all the facts and then you will fall into rejection, anger, or bitterness. You will begin to think that everyone is against you or people are jealous of you. Weariness will cause you to act out in jealousy, which started as a seed planted in your mind that you didn't dismiss.

Many times, I wanted to shut my ministry down because I grew weary waiting on God's promises. Some seasons were harder than others, but I learned to press through. I had to cast down thoughts that were contrary to the Word of God and get back into the presence of the Lord. I had to repent for being selfish and realize that the ministry that God gave me was bigger than me. People are hurting, sick, broken, babes in the faith, depressed, discouraged, and so on. These people are blessed every time I do videos on social media, prophesy, sing, and write new books or blogs. They are looking forward to checking out the message of the day on my social media pages. Even if I wanted to quit, I can't because I'm in too deep and my success determines someone's breakthrough. When I realized the magnitude of the assignment on my life, I renewed my mind immediately and I have to do it daily. I had to focus on the Lord so I wouldn't compare myself to anyone else or get jealous of them. When the enemy whispers, "You are more anointed than that person. You should be up there, not them," just tell the devil, "I don't know what process they had to go through. What God has for me is for me. I will sow a seed into them and support what they are doing." These statements silence the enemy as I resist him and choose to love and rejoice with others. Be a celebrator and not a hater because God sees your heart.

Prophets, make sure your thought life is healthy. Don't entertain demonic ideas because the enemy is the master of perversion. He comes to twist the truth or taint it somehow. We have to learn how to focus on Jesus more than the warfare we are enduring. The enemy sent the attacks against you to wear you out, but you are an overcomer through Jesus. When you get weary, you will forget that you are on the winning side and the promises of God. Remember, God is for you. So who can be against you?

I decree Philippians 4:7, "That the peace of God, which transcends all understanding, will guard my heart and mind in Christ Jesus."

I rebuke the devil from speaking to me in Jesus' name.

I bind up the tormentor that will try to come against my mind in Jesus' name.

I decree that I will think thoughts that glorify the Lord.

Lord, uproot any demonic seeds in my mind.

I plead the blood of Jesus on my mind.

I decree Romans 12:2, "That I will not be conformed to the pattern of this world, but be transformed by the renewing of my mind."

I decree 1 Corinthian 2:16, "That I have on the mind of Christ."

I decree Philippians 2:5, "That I have the same mindset as Jesus."

I decree Hebrews 8:10, "That the Word of God is in my mind and written in my heart."

I decree that I will be sober-minded.

I decree Isaiah 26:3, "That You will keep me in perfect peace because my mind stays on you."

I decree 2 Corinthians 10:5, "I cast down every high imagination that exalts itself against the knowledge of God and bring every thought captive unto the obedience of Jesus Christ."

I decree Colossians 3:2, "That I will set my mind on things above and not on earthly things."

I decree that I have a sound mind.

I decree Philippians 4:8, "That I will think on whatever is true, honest, just, pure, lovely, things of a good report, virtue, or praise."

5

Eyes

Ecclesiastes 1:8 (NASB) says, "All things are wearisome; Man is not able to tell it. The eye is not satisfied with seeing, Nor is the ear filled with hearing."

DID YOU KNOW THAT when you are weary, your spiritual sight is impaired? You have a hard time seeing past the distractions or the thing that is causing you stress. When this occurs, you don't see what God wants or what He is doing. As a result, your perception is altered causing you to miss out on God's heart and mind. The Scripture above explains when things get tough, hard, or when boredom sets in, then your vision can't discern what's in front of you properly. For instance, during the Covid-19 Pandemic in 2020, many prophets were weary and they failed to see the spiritual awakening manifesting. On the Lifetime movie network, there were salvation commercials, which was odd because that channel never played anything about accepting Jesus prior. News channels and newscasters were posting Scriptures on the air and even bringing on preachers to pray. Las Vegas, Nevada, which is known as 'Sin City,' put Scriptures upon their towers and billboards. If you ever visited Vegas, you would know that those billboards are covered in ads promoting sex, strippers, alcohol, gambling, or money. Lastly, there were people all over the globe who were down on their knees crying out to God and repenting. The weary prophets had no idea of the harvest of souls that were coming to the Kingdom of God. They made statements publicly that they got caught up in doing ministry, they fell out of love with God, they used the lockdown of 2020 as their self-reflection period, and that they missed the warning of coronavirus before it came. Their weariness caused them to panic and stress, while those who trusted in the Lord had peace because they knew that God would take care of them.

An example of a prophet who was weary and they couldn't see is Jonah. He had spent a few nights in the belly of fish due to his disobedience. Once the fish vomited him up on the shore, he did what the Lord told him. Yet his heart wasn't in the right place because he got mad when the Ninevites took heed to his prophecy and repented. Jonah failed to see the spiritual awakening before him. Instead, he got upset that God didn't destroy them and he became angrier when a worm ate the leaf that was providing him shade (Jonah 1-4). I believe Jonah got weary in his assignment because he didn't want to witness to people who were different from him. When God gives us a mission, we can't shrink back.

Prophets must see so they can be a watchman on the wall that is constantly sounding the alarm against demonic attacks (Ezekiel 33). The Lord tested Jeremiah twice with his sight before He even used him (Jeremiah 1:11-19). God had to make sure that Jeremiah could see properly and get the correct interpretation. When Jeremiah said that he saw an olive tree and a boiling pot, God told him that he saw well. As a result, the interpretation came of the images. How many times have you missed what God was trying to show you because you were emotional? Honestly, I missed these critical lessons because I was broken, stressed, and dealing with depression when I was on probation before. What the Lord was showing me had to filter through my wounded soul. It wasn't until I received deliverance from the emotional trauma that I was able to see deeper into the spirit realm. For instance, one day someone came to me that was dealing with demonic spirits. I was in a great place mentally and emotionally. The Lord showed me the inside of someone's bathroom and the source of the demonic infiltration. When I saw the hidden things in the spirit, then I knew what to pray against, and the Lord brought this individual great deliverance. Had I been distracted by the trials that I was going through, then I probably wouldn't have been as effective doing ministry.

Just as God had to make sure that Jeremiah could see before He really started using him, He must do the same thing with us. When weariness sets in, you can want something so bad that you will imagine things that aren't even in the will of God for your life. Perhaps, You will start to fantasize about marrying the wrong person, traveling to the wrong places, doing the wrong things, or connecting with the wrong people. The sad part is that you don't recognize that these things are wrong because your flesh wants them so bad that you do anything to get them. For example, many prophetic women have publicly said that a well-known prophet was their husband. They did videos saying that they dreamed of their wedding, having his children, and other things. Just think about it. Someone is lying. God will not give ten women the same husband. These women were weary in their waiting process of marriage and settled by placing their sight on a man that they will never have.

Prophets must yield their emotions to God and allow Him to heal their hearts, so when they go into prayer that can see what God is showing them. Bless are the pure in heart for they will SEE God. I would even add for they will SEE what God is showing them because again their heart is pure and the image doesn't have to filter through bondage (pride, rebellion, fear, lust, perversion, weariness, heartbreak, rejection, etc.). Our sight also applies to the Word of God. When you read the Bible distracted by the cares of this world, it's difficult to receive supernatural revelation. You will miss what the Holy Spirit wants to highlight to you because you are worried about relationships, opportunities, finances, food, etc. However, if you come before the Lord totally devoted unto Him and placing everything on the altar, you will be more likely to receive what the Lord wants you to see. Don't take the bait of only seeing the negatives but look deep in the spirit to see what's to come. God has an amazing plan just for you. Refuse to allow weariness to hinder your sight.

HOW TO SEE IN THE SPIRIT

1. Pray for a Pure heart (Matthew 5:8)

2. Pray that God enlightens your understanding (Ephesians 1:18)
3. Get in the Presence of God
4. Remove distractions

I decree Matthew 6:22, that my eyes are healthy, full of light since it's the lamp of my body.

I decree Psalm 101:3, that I will not set anything worthless before my eyes.

Lord, open my eyes so I can behold wondrous things out of your law (Psalm 119:18).

Lord, open up my eyes so I can see what you are showing me.

Lord, turn my eyes from looking at worthless things (Psalm 119:37).

Lord, enlighten the eyes of my understanding (Ephesians 1:18).

I decree Hebrews 12:2, that I will look to Jesus, who is the author and finisher of my faith.

I decree 2 Corinthians 4:18, that I will not look to things that are seen but to the things that are unseen.

I decree Proverbs 22:9, that I have bountiful eyes and that I will be blessed.

I decree that I will not be wise in my own eyes (Isaiah 5:21).

I decree Psalm 121:1, that I will lift my eyes up to the hills from where my help comes from.

Lord, bless me to see You in the midst of the storm.

Lord, bless me to stay positive and be an encourager when things look bleak.

Lord, bless me to look at my circumstances through the eyes of faith.

Lord, remove any spiritual scales from my eyes so I can see deeper in the spirit realm.

6

Ears

Ecclesiastes 1:8 (NASB) says, "All things are wearisome; Man is not able to tell it. The eye is not satisfied with seeing, Nor is the ear filled with hearing."

WE NEED TO HEAR God because some circumstances are life or death, failure or success, and victory or defeat. A prophet who can't hear God is a disaster waiting to happen because they are God's mouthpiece . They have been set apart to sound the alarm, equip, impart, encourage, and so much more. I am thankful for the times when I heard God's warnings because it saved me from heartache and financial loss. Several things happen to a prophet's hearing when they grow weary:

1. They aren't sharp spiritually
2. They take the voice of God for granted
3. Their flesh speaks
4. They are exhausted physically, mentally, and emotionally
5. They miss out on divine instructions
6. They get into danger.

Let's explore each one.

First, when we get weary, we aren't as sharp spiritually. Weariness can blunt your sensitivity to God and your spiritual senses, especially hearing God's voice. When you have been in a storm for a while, you get tired resulting in a loss of sharpness. You can perform and give your best at something when you are well-rested. Imagine being in a boxing ring fighting with all of your strength. As time passes, fatigue sets in and you find yourself needing to rest. If you aren't able to take a break to recuperate, then you find yourself making mistakes and allowing your component to easily defeat you. You could swing and kick, but the reality is that you aren't able to focus because of the mental, physical, and emotional exhaustion. Your senses are impaired and you are in another zone fighting as you lose control of the fight. Had you been resting and prepared, your senses would be on high alert to win the battle beforehand without getting blind-sighted. This is how a prophet who has grown tired with all the cares of this life becomes. They are consumed with various things such as family, business, finances, etc. while Jesus is on the back burner. They forgot about what God has said or start to question what they hear. They find themselves flustered and wanting to give up. When they enter into prayer, they discover that they aren't hearing from God like they used to. Their ears have become dull and if they aren't careful, their flesh will begin to speak to them. Does this describe you? You want to hear God more, but you realized that you aren't in a posture to do so. Perhaps distraction set in or carnality. You have to press and encourage yourself in the Lord.

Next, a weary prophet can take the voice of God for granted. It's a blessing to hear from God. Many people desire to have the Creator of the universe speak to them regularly. An example of taking God's voice for granted is the following. You could hear prophecies all day, but you find yourself saying, "I don't need another prophecy. I need manifestations." Whenever you keep getting the same words repeatedly is a sign that your promises are closer than ever. For instance, when I was single and waiting for my husband to come, I was growing weary. I couldn't get on social media on holidays, especially Valentine's Day because I felt lonely. I purposely cut off my phone those days for a little while to pray and encourage myself to wait on God to fulfill His promises. Before my husband entered my life, I had dozens of prophecies that my husband was coming and marriage was on the way. Then suddenly, I met this amazing man who adored me and we fell in love. During those weary moments, I didn't realize that I shut out God's voice because I didn't want to hear another word about a husband. God was patient with me and extended His mercy. He kept speaking and I had to do a heart alignment. The Bible warns us to not despise prophecy. Instead of me complaining about me getting the same Word, I changed my perspective. I realized that God was trying to encourage me and let me know that He was about to bless me with my heart's desires. He wanted me to prepare myself because the blessing was approaching. Thank God for what He is about to do in your life. He loves you more than you could ever know. Don't take Him for granted.

Thirdly, the flesh of a weary prophet can speak to them or their flesh can tell them what they want to hear. Have you ever told yourself something that you wanted to hear and mistaken it for the voice of God? Don't feel bad. It was a lesson that you had to learn. I have counseled many women who mistaken the voice of the Lord for theirs concerning their husbands. One woman said that God told her that a prophet on television was her husband. I knew it was false because several other women told others in my circle the same thing. God will never give you someone else's spouse. Having idols in our heart or desiring something more than God can set our flesh to speak deceiving things to us. King Ahab dealt with four hundred lying prophets telling him he was going to win the war because that was an idol in his heart (1 Kings 22:6). When I was waiting on my husband to come, I had to repent of wanting marriage more than God. It wasn't until I took my focus off getting married and fell deeper in love with Jesus that I started to hear the voice of God clearly. I didn't have to doubt if I was hearing my voice or the Lord's voice. I knew that I was hearing on the right frequency because every idol in my heart was removed. I confessed, "Lord, I want you more than I want a husband." Then I became content in my singleness.

Fourthly, God doesn't want us to be exhausted mentally, physically, or emotionally. Rest in Him. Renew your mind daily. Rebuke any doubt, unbelief, and double-mindedness. Think about the promises in the Word and reflect on personal prophecies. When the enemy comes to attack your mind, you can cast demonic thoughts down. Then encourage yourself with all the wonderful things the Lord has done and will do for you very soon.

We have to make sure that we don't burn out by trying to do things in our strength. We need God and must realize that He is our source for everything. The promises that God has planned for you can't be done only by your hand. You will need divine intervention or God's help. Don't worry at night. Go to bed and give the burden to God. I will never forget that God told me one time while I was being attacked in my relationships to go to bed. Initially, my flesh didn't want to sleep because I wanted to pray all night about the situation. However, I used my faith and obeyed God. I trusted Him to do what He said, even though the opposite was occurring. Miraculously in the morning, God worked everything out and I received a breakthrough. The devil was defeated as the Lord Jesus was glorified. Don't miss out on God's instructions because you allow weariness to overwhelm you. I had to decide if I was going to cry all night or trust God. Will you trust God in your situation? Many people are battle fatigued, but they don't have to be because the battle that we are fighting is the Lord's.

Crying all day is emotionally exhausting. After you spend all that time crying, the problem is most likely still there. It's better to pray and focus on God while He starts moving on your behalf. When you are emotionally exhausted, you need to allow God to heal your heart. Don't tell yourself a false prophecy to feel better. Focus on getting close to the Lord because He is our strong tower. The righteous can run in the safety of His arms as He shields us from the cares of this world and gives us supernatural strength to carry on. Don't make the mistake of getting ahead of God when you don't have a solid answer. You need to hear from God and pray about everything that you do. Don't allow your emotions to run your life. We must be spirit-led, so we don't fulfill the lusts of our flesh.

Next, when a prophet is weary, they could miss out on divine instructions. Prophets must be able to hear the voice of the Lord regularly to guide their steps. Imagine if there was a fork in the road. To the right, a mansion and prosperity awaited. To the left were heartache and tragedy. Based on hearing God, the prophet would choose the better option and follow any instructions given, so they know what to expect. There are many decisions that we will need divine instructions to receive everything that the Lord has for us. If we are weary, we might spend less time in prayer and find ourselves consumed with other things. We can't miss those divine moments, especially for our next season. As a result, we go down paths that the Lord never intended for us to travel. Have you been distracted? Sometimes in prayer, you have to rebuke other things from coming into your mind, such as what you will eat for dinner, what's on television, games, what your friend is doing, etc. He who has an ear to hear is what we must declare over ourselves daily. We need to hear God's voice during these last and evil days. For instance, in the Covid-19 pandemic, many pastors opened up their churches because of zeal not because God instructed them too. As a result, many members of their congregation got infected with the virus and some died. Had the pastor sought God and got instructions, then lives would've been spared as they reopened.

Lastly, when a prophet is weary, they could be in danger of losing faith or backsliding. Have you ever witnessed someone who is newly saved? They are excited about Jesus and on fire for the things of God. Most tell everyone that they know about their salvation. However, down the road, they lost their passion and didn't put forth the same effort they did in the beginning. Does this sound like you? Have you fallen out of love with God? It's heartbreaking to see someone walk away from the faith. They went from being passionate about Jesus to not believing in Him. For example, a pastor in a small South Carolina town goes around preaching that God doesn't heal. He believes this because his mother died of cancer and several other saints had passed when he prayed for their healing. I believe he grew weary in his faith and said, "I just don't believe anymore." We can't doubt God and expect Him to answer our prayers. A double-minded person shouldn't expect to receive anything from the Lord (James 1:7). We have to live by faith as the righteous of Jesus Christ. It's a requirement, not an option. Another example is a lady I used to be friends with grew weary in her marriage after a decade of abuse. Her husband divorced her and she became very angry at God. She blamed Him for not restoring her marriage. Instead of standing onto God's promises of restoration, she walked away from the faith and went into another religion. God can't be manipulated or controlled. We must trust His plans. God wants our marriages to be blessed. He wants us to have happy homes. It's not the will of God to have toxic relationships. However, that is all some people know, so they settle and get comfortable in bad situations. God can deliver, save, restore, and bless marriages. He doesn't want the husband to beat on the wife. Sadly, the lady felt that her husband loved her because he hit her sometimes. Domestic violence is not okay. Get somewhere safe and allow God to work on your spouse if you are dealing with an abusive spouse. If people walk away, your relationship with God should remain. Don't let weariness cause you to throw in the towel. Fight this good fight of faith.

Now that we have covered how weariness can affect our hearing. Let's discuss how to get free, so we can hear the voice of the Lord clearly. Follow the steps below and you are on your journey to wholeness.

SOLUTION

1. Repent for having idols or placing things before God, that is the first step to sharpening your hearing.
2. Secondly, worship and enter into the presence of the Lord.
3. Thirdly, bind up your flesh or deceiving spirits from talking to you.
4. Fourth, declare that you are the Lord's sheep and you know His voice. You will not follow any other voices except His.
5. Lastly, ask the Lord to reveal His heart over your life.

Lord, open up my ears to hear Your still small voice.

I bind up weariness from blocking me from hearing God's voice.

I decree that I will incline my ears to hear the voice of the Lord.

I decree Proverbs 18:15 that my ears are one of the wise that seeks knowledge.

I decree Deuteronomy 29:4 that the Lord has given me a heart to know, eyes to see, and ears to hear.

I decree that I will hear what the Lord speaks and follow His commands.

I bind up my ears from being tickled by false prophecy or words from my flesh.

I decree that my ears are blessed because they hear what the Lord has spoken.

I decree Revelations 3:22 that I have an ear to hear what the Spirit of the Lord is speaking to the church.

Lord, bless my ears to be on the right frequency to always hear Your voice.

Lord, bless me to get in the right posture so I can hear Your voice.

Lord, remove any idols in my heart so I can only hear Your voice.

I bind up any deceiving or lying spirits that will try to speak to me in the name of Jesus.

I decree that the only voice I will hear is the voice of the Holy Spirit.

Lord, You are my Shepherd. I am Your Sheep. I know and follow Your Voice.

I decree Isaiah 50:4 that morning by morning God awakens my ear to hear as those who are taught.

7

Mouth

Isaiah 50:4 says, "The Lord GOD hath given me the tongue of the learned, that I should know how to speak a word in season to him that is weary: he wakeneth morning by morning, he wakeneth mine ear to hear as the learned."

GOD DESIRES FOR HIS prophets to have the tongue of the learned. In other words, God wants to instruct and even command us on what to speak. Why? There are so many people around us that are hurting, lost, and need a Savior. You may be tired, but you have to realize that it's not about you. Your assignment and the mandate on your life is far greater than any light momentary affliction. There were times when I wanted to walk away because I felt discouraged but the burden of my assignment was too great and I was in too deep to quit. The realization kicked in when I picked up my phone, opened up my laptop, or checked my PO BOX and saw the prayer request, needed counsel, or the testimony. I can recall me saying, "I can't quit because this ministry is a lifeline to so many people. They come here and God blesses their lives." In those trying moments, God gave me a word to speak to others who were weary, not knowing that as I encouraged others, I was being delivered in the process. Weariness can cause prophets to speak negatively, discourage others, and complain.

Whenever we get weary, we speak things out of our mouths that can negate our prayers, grieve the Holy Spirit, or hurt others. Let's be real. When things got tough have you ever said, "I give up. It's too hard. I quit. Forget it?" I have before and failed to realize that I was my worst enemy. I was the reason why there was a delay to the answer to my prayers. I was speaking the wrong things out of my mouth. Proverbs 18:21 tells us that life and death lies in the power of the tongue. You give something life or build it up by your words. Contrarily, you destroy or cause death by what you speak. Imagine a beautiful altar waiting to be assembled. Whether it's properly constructed depends on what's coming out of your mouth. That's how life is. Our words determine the course of our life and we have the power to change things, especially when something is spoken in faith.

The kingdom of God is voice-activated. God spoke the world into existence. In Genesis 1, we see a pattern of God speaking and He saw a manifestation of His spoken word. We have the Holy Spirit living inside of us that has granted us the same ability to create something out of nothing as we speak in faith. For instance, I spoke the opposite of what I was feeling one day in my wilderness season. I was broken and felt so heavy. I decided to put my faith to the test and call those things that be not as if they were (Romans 4:17). After fifteen minutes of confessing that I was happy and joyful, peace saturated my atmosphere and the burdens were lifted. Another time, I saw the opposite of what happens when negative words are spoken. My ex-husband and I were joking about who would cheat on each other first. Well, a few years into the marriage, those words came back to bite us and infidelity occurred.

Prophets, don't speak negatively when you are weary. You have to use your faith even when you want to withdraw and go back into a spiritual cave. You are God's mouthpiece which is a big responsibility. Your words have power and you are called to shift the atmosphere. When you speak negativity, you must do a heart check.

> *Luke 6:45 (NKJV) says, "A good man out of the good treasure of his heart brings forth good; and an evil man out of the evil treasure of his heart brings forth evil. For out of the abundance of the heart his mouth speaks."*

Whatever is in your heart will determine what you are speaking. It's time to repent for any unforgiveness, bitterness, pride, envy, anger, lust, etc. that is inside of you. If you are unsure if you need deliverance in this area, then step back and reevaluate your words. Are you speaking the opposite of God's word? Are you doubting the prophecy over your life or others' lives? Are you reacting first without thinking things through? Are you speaking whatever comes to your mind? Weariness can cause you to do all these things.

Be careful not to blurt the first thing that comes to your mind or how you feel. That is a sign of a lack of wisdom (Proverbs

17:28). We must be slow to speak (James 1:19). Listen to the facts or give your mind time to process all the information so you won't be quick to be angry. Don't speak your feelings but speak the word of God. What is the Lord saying about your circumstances? Who will you listen to, your flesh or God? Rise up prophet and fight this good fight of faith. Shake off the heaviness and declare what the Lord has proclaimed in the earth. Lives are at stake and you will give an account for every idle word that you have spoken (Matthew 12:36).

Prophets must also be careful not to discourage others. Prophecy is to edify, exhort, and comfort (1 Corinthians 14:3) not to discourage or hurt people, making them feel worse when they come into contact with you. Misery loves company but that doesn't have to be your story. You must get in the presence of God and receive comfort so you can impart it to others.

> *2 Corinthians 1:3-4 says, "Blessed be the God and Father of our Lord Jesus Christ, the Father of mercies and God of all comfort, who comforts us in all our tribulation, that we may be able to comfort those who are in any trouble, with the comfort with which we ourselves are comforted by God."*

Don't curse but bless so you can obtain a blessing (Romans 12:14; 1 Peter 3:9). Lastly, when a prophet gets weary, they start complaining which delays what God wants to do in them and through them. The children of Israel started complaining while they were in the wilderness. As a result, Moses was sick of their complaints and he ended up striking the rock instead of speaking to it (Numbers 20). In other words, he disobeyed God and couldn't enter the Promised Land. Weariness will cause you to disobey God, rebel, and miss out on your blessing. Take heed prophet or lest you will fall (1 Corinthians 10:12).

SOLUTION

1. Pray for the tongue of the learned
   - Ask God what to say
   - Remember God knows how to turn hearts and draw people to Himself
   - God can break barriers and strongholds with His Word

2. Pray for the right company to help, encourage, and influence what you speak
   - You need the right people to pour into you
   - Bad company corrupts good morals (1 Corinthians 15:33)

3. If you don't know what to say then be quiet and wait on God
   - Everything doesn't need to be spoken right now. Take a step back. Make sure things are done in the right spirit.
   - Allow God to fill your mouth

4. Speak faith
   - Faith isn't a feeling
   - You can't please God without faith (Hebrews 11:6)

5. Spend time with God
   - The more time you spend with God, the more attributes of His you will pick up
   - God calls those things that be not as if they were

6. Comfort others so you can be comforted
   - If you feel weary, go minister to someone else. You will feel better.
   - You will reap what you sow. You will be surprised at how much encouragement comes your way in trying times when you have sown into it.

I decree Exodus 4:12 that God will be with my mouth and teach me what I shall say.

Lord, a good word will make my heart glad (Proverbs 12:25).

I decree Proverbs 15:23 that a man has joy by the answer of his mouth. A word spoken in due season is so good.

The Lord GOD has given me the tongue of the learned, that I should know how to speak a word in season to him that is weary (Isaiah 50:4).

I decree that I will speak positive affirmation instead of negative ones.

I decree that I will be careful of the words that I speak.

I decree that I will be slow to speak in Jesus' name.

I yield my mouth to you, Lord.

I decree that I will speak words that edify grace to the hearer.

Lord, set a guard over my mouth (Psalm 141:3).

Lord, keep the door of my lips (Psalm 141:3).

I decree Psalm 34:13 that the Lord will keep my tongue from evil and my lips from deceitful speech.

I decree Psalm 39:1 that I will watch my ways, so I don't sin with my tongue.

8

Heart

Proverbs 13:12 (NKJV) says, "Hope deferred makes the heart sick, But when the desire comes, it is a tree of life."

THERE IS NOTHING WORSE than a wounded prophet because their prophecies indicate the hurt from their soul. Waiting on God's promises can make your heart sorrowful when it seems like it will never happen. When you get tired by the trials in life, you must guard your heart against hurt and bitterness. Proverbs 4:23 (NLT) says, "Guard your heart above all else, for it determines the course of your life." Protecting our hearts should be a top priority because God looks at our hearts (1 Samuel 16:7) and it determines how we respond and think in certain situations. Let's look at the same Scripture in the Good News Translation.

Proverbs 4:23 (GNT) says, " Be careful how you think; your life is shaped by your thoughts."

When weariness sets in, you are more vulnerable to demonic attacks and you must be cautious to keep a pure heart.

For instance, imagine waiting for many years for something to happen, such as getting married, having children, receiving a promotion, opportunities, receiving gifts, etc. You prayed, fasted, and believed but had no breakthrough or manifestations. Then all of a sudden, you see someone receive the very thing that you desire, and you feel that they don't deserve it, haven't earned it, or didn't work hard to receive it. Your flesh or heart naturally wants to get jealous but you must come against those feelings. You must rebuke these thoughts because if you don't, then you could fall away from the faith, mistreat people, walk around wounded, carry unforgiveness, blame God, speak negative words, and stop walking in destiny. Let's explore the effects on your heart when weariness sets in.

1. Walk Away From the Faith

The enemy desires for us to quit and walk away from the Lord Jesus Christ. God will give us strength if we don't quit. On this journey with the Lord, we will face many hardships. We will go through persecution for Jesus's sake. We will experience much warfare. However, we can't shrink back, but we must endure and fight the good fight of faith. When you are feeling weary, it's time to do a heart check to make sure your motives are right. Why are you in ministry? Why are you serving the Lord? Why do you want certain gifts or positions? Will you still serve God when things get tough? Do you love God more than the things in the world?

> *2 Timothy 4:9-10 (ESV) says, "For Demas, in love with this present world, has deserted me and gone to Thessalonica."*

Demas was once a believer in Jesus Christ, but he had a spirit of carnality. He chose worldly pleasures and comfort over God. He abandoned Apostle Paul when he needed him the most. He turned his back on God. When you look at how much Apostle Paul suffered (2 Corinthians 11:16-33), you will see that he was committed to the Lord. Things weren't always easy for him, but he persevered. We must not be like Demas and quit during the storms. We must die to ourselves daily and take up our crosses and follow Jesus (Luke 9:23). The enemy doesn't want you to walk in destiny.

2. Mistreating People

When you get weary, you have to be careful not to mistreat people. For instance, you might have a frustrating day at work and when you come home, you take it out on your family. They don't deserve your wrath and it's not their fault that you are tired of your job. We have to release everything in our hearts unto the Lord.

Cain was a farmer and it takes time to yield a harvest. First, the ground must be tilled. The seed must be planted, watered, get proper sunlight, and protected from pests. Farming is a laborious task. Perhaps Cain felt like he worked harder than his brother Abel who was a shepherd and resented him when God rejected his offering. We can't have an obligated mentality and we must make sure that there is no competition in our hearts. Cain killed his brother because he allowed anger to grow to bitterness, which eventually manifested murder. God gave him a chance to repent by warning him of the sin that was waiting at the door. However, Cain didn't take heed and gave into sin.

> *Genesis 4:7 (NKJV) says, "If you do well, will you not be accepted? And if you do not do well, sin lies at the door. And its desire is for you, but you should rule over it."*

3. Walking Wounded

Weariness can cause people to walk around wounded, carrying unforgiveness and bitterness. When this occurs, you might feel the need to isolate yourself, making yourself more vulnerable to demonic attacks. The enemy loves to get us alone and cut us off from the body of Christ.

> *Hebrews 10:25 (NASB) says, "Not forsaking our own assembling together, as is the habit of some, but encouraging one another; and all the more as you see the day drawing near."*

The devil will plant seeds in our minds, such as, "No one cares about you. No one understands you." However, that's not true. We can't withdraw because we need one another.

> *Ecclesiastes 4:9-11 (ESV) says, "Two are better than one, because they have a good reward for their toil. For if they fall, one will lift up his fellow. But woe to him who is alone when he falls and has not another to lift him up! Again, if two lie together, they keep warm, but how can one keep warm alone?"*

After Peter denied Jesus three times, he walked around wounded. He carried guilt and shame. Jesus had mercy on him and restored him (John 21:15-17).

Perhaps Jeremiah was wounded due to the heaviness of his assignment. We find him often weeping over people's sin and captivity.

Jeremiah 13:17 (NLT) says, "And if you still refuse to listen, I will weep alone because of your pride. My eyes will overflow with tears, because the LORD's flock will be led away into exile."

Jeremiah 9:1 (BSB) says, "Oh, that my head were a spring of water, and my eyes a fountain of tears, I would weep day and night over the slain daughter of my people."

Jeremiah 14:17 (BSB) says, "You are to speak this word to them: "My eyes overflow with tears; day and night they do not cease, for the virgin daughter of my people has been shattered by a crushing blow, a severely grievous wound."

4. Speak Negative

Have you ever spoken the wrong words when you grew weary? Most of us have due to not guarding our hearts and allowing hopelessness to set in (Proverbs 13:12). There is a correlation between the heart and the words that we speak. Out of the abundance of the heart, the mouth speaks (Matthew 12:34;

Luke 6:45). I can recall times when I was hurting and I spoke horrible things that I later regretted. I didn't allow God to heal my heart and took things in my own hands momentarily, only to fail.

In the first book of Ruth, we read about Naomi losing her husband and sons. She grew bitter and blamed God for her suffering. She even lost hope and asked Ruth to call her Mara, which means bitterness[3]. However, Ruth didn't give up on her and God hasn't given up on you. Blaming God for your pain and asking people to call you a name with a terrible meaning is very negative. Naomi had pain deep down in her soul. God eventually restored Naomi's joy and He will do the same for you. Suffering doesn't last always, just hold on.

HOW TO GUARD YOUR HEART

1. Govern your thoughts
   - Don't entertain every thought. Once the seed takes root, then demonic fruit can grow.

2. Get the word of God in your heart
   - Psalm 119:9-11 says, "How can a young man keep his way pure? By guarding it according to your word. With my whole heart I seek you; let me not wander from your commandments! I have stored up your word in my heart, that I might not sin against you."

3. "H4755 - Mara' - Strong's Hebrew Lexicon (KJV)." Blue Letter Bible. Accessed 18 Oct, 2020. https://www.blueletterbible.org//lang/lexicon/lexicon.cfm?Strongs=H4755&t=KJV

3. Release burdens in prayer
    - 1 Peter 5:7 (NKJV) says, "Casting all your care upon Him, for He cares for you."

4. Watch what you say
    - Remember, there is a direct correlation between the heart and the words we speak.
    - Matthew 15:11 (NKJV) says, "Not what goes into the mouth defiles a man; but what comes out of the mouth, this defiles a man."

5. Be a watchman over your heart

    - Be protective over what enters your heart.
    - Proverbs 4:23 says, "Keep thy heart with all diligence; for out of it are the issues of life."

Lord, create in me a pure heart in Jesus' name.

Lord, you warn us that what's coming out of our mouths is an indication of what's in our hearts. Let my words bring glory to you.

Lord, you warn us that the things coming out of our mouth defile us. Bless my heart to have the right motives.

Lord, you look at my heart. I pray that I will be pleasing in your sight.

Lord, you warn us that from the heart come evil thoughts, murder, adultery, sexual immorality, theft, false testimony, and slander (Matthew 15:19; Mark 7:21). These are the reasons why I need you because You are the only One who can set me free of these wicked things.

Lord, you warn us that the good man brings good things out of the good treasures of his heart and the evil man brings evil treasures out of his heart (Luke 6:45). Lord, make me over.

Lord, bless me to get your word deeper into my heart and never forget them so I can teach my children and grandchildren (Deuteronomy 4:9).

Lord, bless me with wisdom and guide my heart on the right course (Proverbs 23:19).

Lord, bless me not to trust in my own heart but trust in You and Your word. You warn me that he that trusts in his own heart is a fool (Proverbs 28:26).

Lord, bless me not to walk around wounded. I will cast all my cares upon you because you care for me.

9

Walk

Colossians 1:10 (NASB) says, "So that you will walk in a manner worthy of the Lord, to please Him in all respects, bearing fruit in every good work and increasing in the knowledge of God."

OUR WALK IS IMPORTANT to God. He longs to direct our steps; that's why He provided His Word (Psalm 119:105). It's critical that our feet are on the right path so we can receive God's best. We don't have time to go to the left or to the right because it can cause us to get off track (Proverbs 4:26-27). The enemy of our soul desires to sift us like wheat and wants us to waiver off the straight path (Proverbs 1:15-16; Isaiah 59:7; Matthew 7:14). The devil wants us to walk an evil path. He desires for our feet to run swiftly to evil (Proverbs 6:18). The steps of a good man are ordered by the Lord (Psalm 37:23). Our feet are beautiful and blessed when we preach the gospel (Isaiah 52:7; Romans 10:14-15). God wants our feet to be like the feet of the hind or mountain deer (2 Samuel 22:32-35; Psalm 18:33-36; Habakkuk 3:19). This animal can jump on mountainous terrain without stumbling (Psalm 121:2-5). Likewise, our feet can overcome the devil's stumbling blocks through Christ. God wants us to have consistency in our faith walk.

Whenever you get weary, your steps can be halted. You were once making progress, but the storms in life diminished your momentum and you stopped moving forward. Be careful. You must push even when you don't feel like it. Whenever we walk in a manner that is pleasing to the Lord, we make the most of every opportunity to do what we are called to do. Our time is short, souls need to be saved, and the gospel of the Lord Jesus must be preached. Don't be occupied by the trials of this life, but put your trust in the Lord. You must know and have total confidence that God will fulfill His promise. Whenever you get weary, you can take the bait of the enemy and go back into the cave or a spiritual low place. Prophets, you must walk as Jesus walked. When prophets get weary in their walk, several things happen such as depression, lack of faith, and going through the motions. Let's discuss each one.

Depression is debilitating and many people deal with it. It's an attack of the enemy to kill our purpose and take the people of God out of this world prematurely. Sadly, many pastors and spiritual leaders have dealt with depression for years. When they didn't get help such as counseling or deliverance, they committed suicide, which was what the enemy wanted. The devil knew that the leader could no longer be a threat to his kingdom when they're dead. Depression can drain your joy and peace.

I was chronically depressed for years. Sometimes the pain would be so intense that I didn't want to live anymore and I wanted it all to be over. I was tired of suffering through the trials. I can recall a time where I laid on my couch for three days. I didn't shower, comb my hair, or eat. I was seeing dark shadows or demons dancing in front of me in my living room. I didn't have the strength to fight them and I didn't even care. I rolled over and tried to sleep my life away. I looked up to heaven and prayed, "Lord, I don't want to live anymore." Suddenly, the Lord spoke, "It's not your time to die yet. You have work to do." Those words started to break the depression off me. Sometime after, my college friend called to check on me. I was avoiding everyone and I wasn't going to answer, but I heard the Lord again speak. "Answer the phone!" As soon as I did, my friend started to pray for a few minutes. I started to get free and the spirit of depression left! After her prayer, she described to me the exact spirits or demons that I had seen previously in my living room. She said they had long claws and sharp teeth trying to attack me. She prayed until she saw them leave out the front door. Soon after, I was able to get on my laptop and write the book that the Lord instructed me to write. Depression hindered me from going forward.

Elijah was a powerful prophet of God. He grew weary, depressed, and wanted to die after being used mightily by God to kill Jezebel's false prophets (1 Kings 18). After we have a huge victory, we should be consistent and be victorious in everything. However, that is not always the case. The enemy will sometimes cause a counter-attack such as backlash or retaliation. Elijah would've been more effective if he had made more progress, killed more false prophets or destroyed the enemy's camp even further in the days to follow. Yet, that didn't happen. Instead, he prayed to die (1 Kings 19:4). God was faithful and didn't allow depression, fear, and weariness to take out His prophet. Can you recall the times when depression was attacking you? You probably didn't want to do much except sleep, eat, or cry. Depression is a destiny killer. Don't shrink back! Take a step forward as a prophetic act! Declare, "I will make progress! Depression will not hinder me in Jesus' name!"

When we get weary, our faith walk suffers. We will find that we no longer have childlike faith where we believe anything the Lord promises without over-analyzing, questioning, or doubting. If you aren't careful, then you will find yourself speaking things contrary to what God has spoken, "It won't happen. You are wasting your time. Just walk away." The Bible makes it clear that there is nothing too hard for God, we can do all things through Christ, and when a righteous man falls seven times, he gets back up again. We are mandated to live a life of faith. The just shall live by faith, meaning it's not an option but a requirement.

After Jesus was crucified, the disciples scattered and their whole world was shaken. Their teacher, who they walked with closely for three years, was no longer around, so they thought. Jesus started appearing to many such as Mary and the two women who were with her. They ran back to tell the disciples that Jesus was alive, but Thomas doubted. His faith wavered and his mind couldn't process what the women were speaking. Perhaps he was weary from the thought of himself being crucified next.

If it happened to Jesus, then it could happen to him since they were connected. Thomas spoke, "I will not believe until I see the nail marks in his hands and put my finger where the nails were and put my hand into his side." A week later, Jesus came into the room supernaturally because the doors were locked shut and He told Thomas to place his fingers in his hands where the nail holes were. Then He told him to put his hands on His side. He then rebuked him for not believing (Luke 20:10-29). Jesus spoke many things that were going to happen to prepare the disciples. Similarly, God speaks things to us to prepare us for what's to come. We can't doubt it even if it seems surreal or outrageous. Walk by faith, not by sight (2 Corinthians 5:7).

Lastly, when we get weary, we tend to go through the motions. In other words, we are withdrawn, no interest is shown, and we forget how important something is. Sometimes the trials in life can make us numb but God never intended for His children to stay in this state long term. God gave us emotions, so it's okay to grieve and when you are done, get back up, and live life. Numbness and a lack of empathy is a sign of a hard heart. We must always make sure we are doing daily heart checks by giving God all the things that may distance us from Him. Going through the motions can put space between God and us when the Word goes in one ear and out the other, when we disobey Him and become consumed with the cares of the world. For instance, the Israelites ignored God, turned their backs on Him, and sinned against Him many times throughout the Bible. When they did hear the Word spoken by the priests or the warnings from the prophets, transformation rarely took place. They choose false gods over the true living God and when they were in bondage, they finally cried out to God for deliverance. God is merciful and kind. He loves us and will do anything for His children. He ended up raising up various deliverers or judges. Then the cycle repeated itself. The Israelites were going through the motions in their faith walk, but as we can see, this is dangerous. We can't become complacent and take the Word of God lightly. Fast and remove anything that you are placing before the Lord. Allow God to refresh you so you can be about His business. We need to care about what He cares about and the things concerning Him.

SOLUTION

1. Walk circumspectly (Ephesians 5:15).
    a. See then that ye walk circumspectly, not as fools, but as wise.
        - Live like the wise
        - Disconnect from the foolishness or bad influences
    b. Don't stand in the path of sinners (Psalm 1:1)
        - Bless is the man that walketh not in the counsel of the ungodly, nor standeth in the way of sinners.
        - Stop taking ungodly advice

2. Pray over your feet.
    a. Our feet should run from evil (Proverbs 6:18)
        - Feet that be swift in running to mischief
    b. Our feet will not get ensnared by Satan's trap (Proverbs 3:26)
        - For the Lord shall be thy confidence, and shall keep thy foot from being taken.

c. Our feet will not fall into the enemy's pit (Proverbs 26:27)
   - Whoso diggeth a pit shall fall therein.

d. Ask God to order your steps

3. Pray for a pure heart.
   a. Hide the Word in your heart, so you don't sin (Psalm 119:11).
      - Thy word have I hid in mine heart, that I might not sin against thee.

4. Keep going forward
   a. No matter what happens, be determined to make progress.
   b. Philippians 3:14 says, "I press toward the mark for the prize of the high calling of God in Christ Jesus."

5. Let the Word cause an illumination of what path to take.
   a. Psalm 119:105 says, "Thy word is a lamp unto my feet, and a light unto my path."
   b. Ask yourself, "If I walk down this path, will the Lord be pleased?"

Lord, watch the paths of my feet so all my ways will be established (Proverbs 4:26).

I decree that my feet will run from evil and not towards it (Proverbs 6:18).

I decree that my feet will stay on God's path and will not slip in Jesus' name (Psalm 17:5).

I decree that I have the law of God in my heart, so my steps will not slip (Psalm 37:31).

Lord, my heart is set on pleasing You. I will not deviate from Your way (Psalm 44:18).

I will restrain my feet from every evil way so that I may keep Your Word (Psalm 119:101).

Lord, I will acknowledge You so You can direct my path (Proverbs 3:6).

Lord, I declare that I will not stand in the path of sinners (Psalm 1:1).

I declare that I won't enter the path of the wicked (Proverbs 4:14).

Lord, make my feet like the hind's feet and set me up on high places (Psalm 18:33).

I decree that I will walk circumspectly in Jesus' name (Ephesians 5:15).

I declare that I will not go to the left or to the right but on the path that you have set before me in Jesus' name (Proverbs 4:26-27).

10

Discernment

1 Corinthians 2:15 says, "But he that is spiritual judgeth all things, yet he himself is judged of no man."

PROPHETS HAVE TO BE spiritual because they are called by Jesus Christ as a gift to the church (Ephesians 4:8-12). They must be spirit-led (Galatians 5:16) because they are friends of God (James 2:23) and the devil hates it. That's why they must be discerning. They can't afford to blend in with the world or have a spirit of carnality (1 John 2:15-17).

Notice the word judgeth in the above Scripture. The Greek word is anakrino (G350), which translates into examine, search, or discern[4]. The same word 'anakrino' is used again for the word discerned in 1 Corinthians 2:14, " But the natural man receiveth not the things of the Spirit of God: for they are foolishness unto him: neither can he know them, because they are

4. "G350 - anakrinō - Strong's Greek Lexicon (KJV)." Blue Letter Bible. Accessed 18 Oct, 2020. https://www.blueletterbible.org//lang/lexicon/lexicon.cfm?Strongs=G350&t=KJV

spiritually discerned." In other words, it takes the Spirit of God to help us understand spiritual things.

A weary prophet might not be able to discern properly or be able to judge all things because they can't see past their current situation. We have to test everything and everyone, especially since there is a spirit of lawlessness running rampant upon the earth. In 2020, there is a defunding of the police movement and a disregard of the law. Many police officers are quitting to choose another career path. If there are no police, then who would come if we dial 911? What happens if a burglar is breaking into our homes and there are no police? Who will help bring order in our society? There is so much disorder all across the globe and prophets have to be beacons of light. Some people have ulterior motives in the midst of the COVID-19 pandemic, the November 3, 2020 election, the Black Lives Matter protests, and why they want to connect with us. Prophets must be able to discern these motives.

We must ask ourselves, "Why does this individual want to connect with us? Why do they want to join our ministry? What is their role in our lives? Who sent them, God or the enemy? Who should I vote for? What are the origins of these movements springing up on the earth?" We must even go further and ask, "What should I be doing in this season? What is on the heart of God? How does the Lord feel about what's happening across the globe? Should I accept this ministry engagement? How does God feel about me connecting with this individual?"

First, let's discuss the 2020 Coronavirus pandemic. The media and certain front line individuals are saying things that later proved to be contradictory to the facts while the Holy Spirit is revealing their deception. Have you ever felt like something wasn't right or there was more to the story while watching the news? It's because the Holy Spirit, the Spirit of truth, reveals all things and what's hidden will be exposed. Or what's done in the dark will come to the light. What's spoken in secret will be made public (Luke 12:2-3). When the virus surfaced in early January 2020, the media lied and said the virus came from a meat market. There was so much confusion as conspiracy theories arose. However, the Holy Spirit showed some of His prophets that the virus was made in the lab. Once, the Lord showed me the genome sequence of the virus sitting on a computer as I prayed, which was confirmed by other prophets. President Trump and Vice President Pence lied to the American people multiple times about the severity of the virus and tried to play it down. However, the Holy Spirit allowed me to discern those lies and I had to stop watching the daily coronavirus task force briefings. Eventually, all these lies were exposed. Many people have died due to a lack of discernment by following the wrong voices and not seeking the counsel of the Lord.

Next, we need discernment in the November 3, 2020 election and any election afterward. We can't just vote all democratic or all republican. We must do our research on each person on the ballot. We need to vote locally because many laws, regulations, or ordinances affect our families and us. Since we have the wrong people in certain offices, we see the following: laws are passed to protect pedophiles, promotion of full-term abortion, pushing of LGBT rights, removing God out of the equation, and other things contrary to the will of God. Now the nation is crying out and appalled at the demonic activity manifesting on our streets. We are suffering due to voting for the wrong candidates and putting them in offices that God never authorized. Some of these people aren't in alignment with God but with the devil.

Proverbs 14:34 says, "Righteousness exalts a nation while sin is a reproach to people." In other words, sin is a disgrace. What's happening is a disgrace in the sight of God. Prophets, it's time to intercede for the lost as the signs of Christ's return are near (Matthew 24). When we are discerning, we aren't looking at someone's exterior being suspicious. We are totally relying on the Holy Spirit, while He reveals the intentions of the person's heart. God will give us the wisdom to search out a matter and research a person's past. Again, the Greek word 'anakrino' also means to search.

Let's now discuss the Black Lives Matter movement. For many centuries, African Americans have been lynched and treated unjustly. Some laws were passed to discriminate against them and prevented them from becoming successful in life. Prophets have the heart of God and stand against injustice. However, the Holy Spirit will warn you if there is a demonic agenda. Prophets must not follow the crowd but follow God. When I first became aware of the Black Lives Matter movement, I felt like something was off and I didn't have peace about it. Whenever you don't have peace about something, pray and ask the Lord, "What is going on?" Later, the truth was revealed about the founders and how they chant to their dead ancestors. One of the founders said that she is invoking their spirits so it can be resurrected and work through her to accomplish the work that needs to be done.[5] That sounds like possession or giving the enemy the legal right to enter your body to take over. God does not want us to communicate with the dead. Also, it's sad to see something that could potentially be a powerful movement be exploited by terrorist groups such as ANTIFA. These groups come in the middle of the protests, destroy property, and loot. Some of these groups paint their faces black to blend in with the African American protestors. What we see isn't a real protest like those of civil rights activists like Dr. Martin King Jr. The protests he led were peaceful, not ones of violence like we see today. Many people are dying daily in these riots and caught COVID in the midst of them. Cars are plowing into the crowds and shooters are randomly shooting protestors. If God didn't instruct you to be on the streets, then you need to stay put. If not, then you are outside of His will and there's no safety.

Lastly, we must discern why people want to connect with us because the devil will go far to deceive us. In 2019, my preaching schedule started to pick up and I was traveling. God knew that I desire to preach His Word across the globe. However, at the end of 2019 and the beginning of 2020, my schedule started to slow down. I was battling discouragement and started to get weary. Don't take the bait of getting into your emotions. Pray! COVID-19 wasn't in the USA yet and many conferences were

5. "Black Lives Matter Is 'a Spiritual Movement,' Says Co-Founder Patrisse Cullors." 2020. Religion News Service. June 15, 2020. https://religionnews.com/2020/06/15/why-black-lives-matter-is-a-spiritual-movement-says-blm-co-founder-patrisse-cullors/.

occurring. I later repented because I realized that God was protecting and preparing me for the pandemic.

One day, I checked my email and it was an invite from a church in the United Kingdom. I also desired to go and I am very knowledgeable of the British Monarchy's history. The enemy knew that, so he tried to scam me. When I got the invite, I was very excited because of the location and the huge honorarium of seven thousand dollars offered to me. I went to the website and it looked authentic. A contract was even sent for me to agree to come. The more I thought about it, I knew it was too good to be true. I had to get out of my feelings and calm down so I could really hear from the Lord. Due to the overwhelming feeling of excitement, I couldn't focus, so I prayed a simple prayer, "Lord, let me be in your will. If this is a scam, please reveal it. If this is legit, then let everything work out." Afterward, I went to bed. When I woke up, I had my answer. The Holy Spirit led me to the email that was sent and highlighted a name that was reorganized out of place. They wanted me to send money to a person who had a weird name instead of an agency to obtain a VISA. Then the Lord led me to Facebook and the person popped up. WOW! The truth was in black and white. The website of the church and the conference was fake. The person was pretending to be someone else. Immediately, I messaged the imposter and exposed him. Then I reported him to several agencies to inform them that this individual is impersonating government officials. What if I didn't pray? What if I allowed the fact that I was discouraged and weary to cloud my discernment? I would have been scammed.

<u>SOLUTION</u>

1. Don't judge by appearance.
   a. John 7:24 says, "Judge not according to the appearance, but judge righteous judgment."
   b. Rely on the Holy Spirit to help you examine or search out a matter.

2. Don't be hasty.
   a. Stop moving ahead of God. If you haven't heard an answer from Him, stay put.
   b. Whoever is hasty or one who moves too quickly will miss their way.
   c. Proverbs 19:2 (ESV) says, "Desire without knowledge is not good, and whoever makes haste with his feet misses his way."

3. Follow God
   a. Just because something is popular doesn't mean God is in it.
   b. People followed Simon the Sorcerer because he had great power.
   c. Acts 8:10 (ESV) says, "They all paid attention to him, from the least to the greatest, saying, "This man is the power of God that is called Great."

4. Determine the source
   a. Is the information or person from above or below? What spirit is in operation?
   b. You will know them by their fruit (Matthew 7:15).

5. Search out everything
    a. Be like the Bereans
    b. Acts 17:11 (EXB) says, "The Bereans ·were eager to hear what Paul and Silas said [L eagerly received the word/message] and ·studied [examined] the Scriptures every day to find out if these things were true [C to confirm Paul's teaching was in line with Scripture]."

I declare that I am spiritual and will judge all things (1 Corinthians 2:15).

Lord, help me to stay discerning so Your plans for my life will not be altered.

Lord, increase the discernment in my life so I will not be led astray.

I decree that I will be discerning and hold on to whatever is good (1 Thessalonians 5:21).

Lord, bless me with wisdom so I can judge for myself what is right (Luke 12:57).

I decree that I will not be destroyed for a lack of knowledge (Hosea 4:6).

I decree that I will look beyond the surface of things (2 Corinthians 10:7).

I decree that I will discern beyond the appearance of things in Jesus' name (John 7:24).

Lord, bless me to have knowledge with the zeal that I carry (Proverbs 19:2).

Lord, bless me not to be so hasty so I don't miss your will for my life (Proverbs 19:2).

Lord, bless me to discern the signs of the times (Matthew 16:3).

Lord, bless Your Word to discern my thoughts and the motives of my heart (Hebrews 4:12).

I decree that I will renew my mind, so I will be able to discern what the will of God is (Romans 12:2).

I decree that I will renew my mind so I can discern what is good, acceptable, and perfect in the sight of God (Romans 12:2).

Lord, bless me to be discerning, so I can test every spirit to see if they are from you or not (1 John 4:1).

Lord, bless me with all discernment so I can be pure and blameless for the day of Christ (Philippians 1:9-10).

Lord, bless my spiritual senses to mature so I can discern between good and evil (Hebrews 5:14).

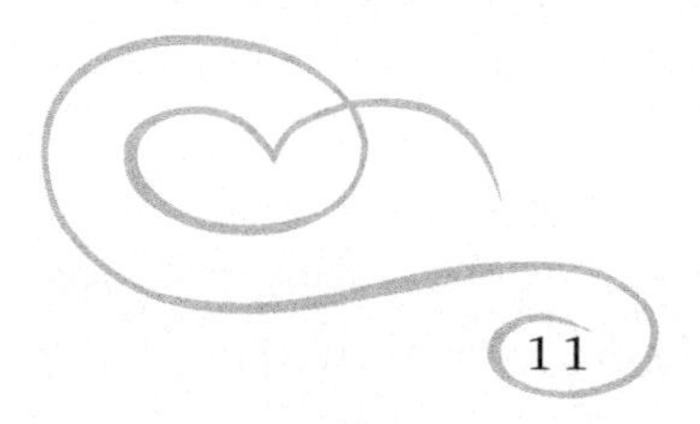

11

Seasons

1 Chronicles 12:32 says, "And of the children of Issachar, which were men that had understanding of the times, to know what Israel ought to do; the heads of them were two hundred; and all their brethren were at their commandment."

THE CHILDREN OR THE sons of Issachar understood the timing of God. They were the descendants of Issachar, who was the son of Leah and Jacob (Genesis 35:23). They knew what Israel should do and the right time to do it. They were knowledgeable of what the Lord was doing. They had great discernment so they could stay in alignment with God's agenda. They had the wisdom of God to be in sync with His Spirit. The Hebrew word for season is "eth[6]. It means occurrences, times, events, occasions, or experiences. God has appointed certain things to happen at an appointed time.

---

6. "H6256 - `eth - Strong's Hebrew Lexicon (KJV)." Blue Letter Bible. Accessed 18 Oct, 2020. https://www.blueletterbible.org//lang/lexicon/lexicon.cfm?Strongs=H6256&t=KJV

The sons of Issachar were in the timing of God. Have you ever done something and became frustrated because you didn't get the results that you desired? Perhaps you followed God's instructions or the vision He gave you, but it was in the wrong season or it wasn't the right time. We must understand that no matter how hard we try, success won't happen in the wrong season. However, as you stay faithful, then you will succeed because you did not give up. God will look upon you and bless the work of your hands. When it's your time, then nothing can stop what God will do for you.

God has given His servants many prophecies about their future and destiny. Sometimes we feel like those prophecies will happen now instead of a later date. As we wait for the manifestations, then weariness can set in. Be faithful as you wait for God's promises because your timing will catch up with God's timing. David was anointed before his time to become king. Imagine being anointed but sitting on the sidelines waiting for your season to come.

Joseph had to wait for his time to reign. He had dreams where his family would bow down to him but in the natural, he was in prison for many years. If Joseph had gotten out of prison before his appointed time, he wouldn't have become the second in command in Egypt. God had him in a holding cell-like many prophets because their appointed time has not come. God has them hidden for a season because He is doing a great inner work.

When I started writing books, no one wanted to purchase them. The first few books were full of errors because I lacked the funds to invest in an editor and had no one to help proofread. I felt weary at times, but the Lord gave me a list of twenty-one books to write. However, at the appointed time, God began to favor my books and people started to buy them. It's amazing to look back and see the growth. Be consistent because your time is coming. Prophets must discern the right timing of open doors, divine connections, walking in different anointings, and when or if to start a family.

Ecclesiastes 3:1-8 explains the various times and seasons for things to happen in our lives.

> *1 To everything there is a season, and a time to every purpose under the heaven:*
>
> *2 A time to be born, and a time to die; a time to plant, and a time to pluck up that which is planted;*
>
> *3 A time to kill, and a time to heal; a time to break down, and a time to build up;*
>
> *4 A time to weep, and a time to laugh; a time to mourn, and a time to dance;*
>
> *5 A time to cast away stones, and a time to gather stones together; a time to embrace, and a time to refrain from embracing;*
>
> *6 A time to get, and a time to lose; a time to keep, and a time to cast away;*
>
> *7 A time to rend, and a time to sew; a time to keep silence, and a time to speak;*

8 A time to love, and a time to hate; a time of war, and a time of peace.

Times and seasons are important to God. When the disciples asked Jesus when he was going to restore the kingdom back to Israel, he replied that only God had the authority to determine the timing and for them not to worry about it (Acts 1:6-7).

God planned every intricate detail when He made creation. The sun and the moon are on a set time for seasons, days, and years. They are lights in the heavens to separate the day and the night (Genesis 1:14).

Psalm 104:19 (ESV) says, "He made the moon to mark the seasons; the sun knows it's time for setting."

Genesis 1:14 (ESV) says, "And God said, "Let there be lights in the expanse of the heavens to separate the day from the night. And let them be for signs and for seasons, and for days and years."

God created the trees to yield fruit at an appointed season (Psalm 1:3). We can look at leaves on a tree and determine the season. For instance, when the green leaves turn brown, then autumn is here. When the leaves are fallen off the trees, then winter is upon us.

Matthew 24:32 (ESV) says, "From the fig tree learn its lesson: as its branch becomes tender and puts out its leaves, you know that summer is near."

When it came to celebrating the Jewish feasts, there were appointed times (Leviticus 23:2,4,37,44). The Israelites had to be in sync with God's timing in order to receive the blessings that were being released.

There were times when I was believing for doors to open, but it wasn't the right time. If the door would have opened for me at that moment, then I could have messed it up because I wasn't prepared or delivered to walk through them. Years ago, a television network contacted me about being on their platform. I knew that I wasn't ready because I was bound by fear and the thought of public speaking nauseated me. I referred an apostle whose ministry I was attending to be featured. His wife and him flew out to Florida to meet with the executives of the network. As a result, he was on television. Had I accepted the invitation, I would've been sick and embarrassed. The anointing wouldn't have flowed. Around that time, I was learning how to flow with the Holy Spirit and could barely preach. I would've slammed the door right in my own face. We have to discern what doors we are to walk through. We must know which opportunities are ours or if the Lord wants us to recommend them to someone else. Remember, the doors will open when God feels like you are ready. When God sends you, demonstrate His Kingdom and don't hold back. Let His glory flow through you and touch the lives around you.

Many of us are weary because it feels like we are overlooked. It doesn't feel good to be rejected. You know you are anointed, but others aren't able to see it. Yet, God knows how to process us. I had the fire of God upon my life for many years and when I first stepped into ministry, no one knew my name. People didn't want to listen to my videos or read my books. The people who were on the major platforms wouldn't give me any time or pay me attention. However, as I stayed the course, God caused the right people to notice me and the works that I am doing. The Lord sent divine connections and allowed the right people to favor me. While you are waiting for connections, be ready to produce the goods. No one will be able to refute who you are in God because you will be able to function in your role or office. Many people may try to deny who you are in God, but if they look at the fruit and the works, then they will see otherwise. Some people have looked at my outer appearance and assumed that I wasn't a prophet, but as they started listening or doing their research, then they could see God in my life. One day I was emotional. I was tired of being in the wilderness. I just wanted to go into a spiritual cave and loathe in depression. However, the Lord wouldn't allow me too. He spoke, "Get on periscope." I wiped my eyes and put on some makeup. I got on periscope and began to minister about prophet Zephaniah. Suddenly, a major minister came on my broadcast and he shared it with his thousands of followers. Immediately, the view count went from twelve people to about four hundred. I was not used to that many people on my broadcast at once. I tried my best to keep a straight face but inside I was overwhelmed with a mixture of emotions. I ended the broadcast early, and when I finished, I fell on my face praising God. I remember saying, "God, you heard my prayer and elevated me." After the apostle shared my broadcast, my following on social media doubled.

Some prophets are weary because they aren't walking in certain anointings. Discerning the time is critical because we must know that God anoints us for specific assignments. For instance, I noticed that when I travel to minister at different events, my assignment is different. Sometimes God tells me to prophesy to everyone there. If I try to do the same thing the next time, it doesn't work or there is no flow of the oil. Other times, God will give me words of knowledge and I have to pray for the sick to be healed. I remember when God gave me a vision of full stadiums and me preaching to the masses. I saw walkers, canes, and wheelchairs everywhere. There were so many miracles, but in reality, I wasn't walking in that type of anointing. Instead of becoming discouraged when I prayed for someone and nothing happened, I let it encourage me. I know one day I will walk in the miracle anointing. For years, I prayed for blind eyes to open and nothing happened. However, as I stayed faithful then the Lord increased the anointing upon my life and the blind started to see when I prayed.

Prophets, you must discern when and if you are to start a family. God didn't allow Prophet Jeremiah to marry or have children. Apostle Paul didn't feel led to marry because he would've been distracted from fulfilling his calling. Plus he had the gift of celibacy (1 Corinthians 7:7). When you marry, you are sharing your personal space with someone else. You can't solely focus on the Lord because you have to divide your attention elsewhere.

1 Corinthians 7: 32-34 says, "[32]The unmarried man is anxious about the things of the Lord, how to please the Lord. [33]

But the married man is anxious about worldly things, how to please his wife, [34] *and his interests are divided."*

Do you know who you are in Christ? Are you established in your calling and assignment? Will you idolize your spouse when they come? These questions must be considered because marriage and starting a family is life changing. If you marry the wrong person, then your destiny will be altered. Samson chose the wrong woman, Delilah, and he ended up losing his life (Judges 13-16). If you have children, you will be busy caring for them.

<u>SOLUTION</u>

1. Pray
   a. We must fast and seek the correct timing. Trust Him to order your steps.
   b. Don't move until God says go.
   c. Don't do stuff because everyone else is doing it. Do what God has for you.

2. Patience
   a. Wait on God because He has something amazing in store for you.
   b. If the answer doesn't come immediately, then pray about it and sleep on it. Sometimes the answer doesn't come until you wake up.

3. Do you have peace about it?
   a. If you have peace about it then it's a sign of God's approval.

b. If you feel uneasy about something then maybe it's not the right timing.

Lord, bless me to have an understanding of the times and seasons like the sons of Issachar.

Lord, bless me to be sensitive to Your divine timing.

Lord, bless me to be patient and not get ahead of You.

Lord, You warn us that there is a season for everything. Help me to discern the current season of the nation and the church.

Lord, You change the times and seasons. You remove kings and set up kings. You give wisdom to the wise and knowledge to those who have an understanding (Daniel 2:21).

I decree that I will be faithful as I wait for Your promises Lord.

I decree that I will reap a mighty harvest because while the earth remains so does seedtime and harvest (Genesis 8:22).

I decree that I will not grow weary of well doing because I will reap an abundant harvest if I faint not (Galatians 6:9).

Lord, bless me to be knowledgeable of what You are doing.

Lord, bless me with great discernment so I can stay in alignment with Your agenda.

Lord, bless me with godly wisdom so I can be in sync with Your Spirit.

About The Author

KIMBERLY MOSES STARTED OFF her ministry as Kimberly Hargraves. She is highly sought after as a prophetic voice, intercessor and prolific author. There is no doubt that she has a global mandate on her life to serve the nations of the world by spreading the Gospel of Jesus Christ. She has a quickly expanding worldwide healing and deliverance ministry. Kimberly Moses wears many hats to fulfill the call God has placed on her life as an entrepreneur over several businesses including her own personal brand Rejoice Essentials which promotes the Gospel of Jesus Christ.

She also serves as a life coach and mentor tomany women. She is also the loving mother of two wonderful children. She is married to Tron. Kimberly has dedicated her life to the work of ministry and to serve others under the call God has placed over her life. Kimberly currently resides in South Carolina.

She is a very anointed woman of God who signs, miracles and wonders follow. The miraculous and incessant testimonies attributed to her ministry are incalculable, with many reporting physical and mental healing, financial breakthroughs, debt cancellations and other favorable outcomes. She is known across the globe as a servant who truly labors on behalf of God's people through intercession.

She is the author of The Following:

"Overcoming Difficult Life Experiences with Scriptures and Prayers"
"Overcoming Emotions with Prayers"
"Daily Prayers That Bring Changes"
"In Right Standing,"
"Obedience Is Key,"
"Prayers That Break The Yoke Of The Enemy: A Book Of Declarations,"
"Prayers That Demolish Demonic Strongholds: A Book Of Declarations,"
"Work Smarter. Not Harder. A Book Of Declarations For The Workforce,"
"Set The Captives Free: A Book Of Deliverance."
"Pray More Challenge"
"Walk By Faith: A Daily Devotional"
"Empowering The New Me: Fifty Tips To Becoming A Godly Woman"
"School of the Prophets: A Curriculum For Success"
"8 Keys To Accessing The Supernatural"
"Conquering The Mind: A Daily Devotional"
"Enhancing The Prophetic In You"
"The ABCs of The Prophetic: Prophetic Characteristics"
"Wisdom Is The Principal Thing: A Daily Devotional"
"It Cost Me Everything"

"The Making Of A Prophet: Women Walking in Prophetic Destiny"
"The Art of Meditation: A Daily Devotional"
"Warfare Strategies: Biblical Weapons"
"Becoming A Better You"
"I Almost Died"
"The Pastor's Secret: The D.L. Series"
"June Bug The Busy Bee: The Gamer"
"June Bug The Busy Bee: The Bully"

You can find more about Kimberly at
www.kimberlyhargraves.com

For Rejoice Essential Magazine, visit
www.rejoiceessential.com

For beauty and t-shirts, visit
www.rejoicingbeauty.com

Please write a review for my books on Amazon.com

Support this ministry:
Cashapp: $ProphetessKim
Paypal.me/remag

References

1. "G1573 - ekkakeo - Strong's Greek Lexicon (KJV)." Blue Letter Bible. Accessed 18 Oct, 2020. https://www.blueletterbible.org//lang/lexicon/lexicon.cfm?Strongs=G1573&t=KJV
2. "H348 - 'Iyzebel - Strong's Hebrew Lexicon (KJV)." Blue Letter Bible. Accessed 18 Oct, 2020. https://www.blueletterbible.org//lang/lexicon/lexicon.cfm?Strongs=H348&t=KJV
3. "H4755 - Mara' - Strong's Hebrew Lexicon (KJV)." Blue Letter Bible. Accessed 18 Oct, 2020. https://www.blueletterbible.org//lang/lexicon/lexicon.cfm?Strongs=H4755&t=KJV
4. "G350 - anakrino - Strong's Greek Lexicon (KJV)." Blue Letter Bible. Accessed 18 Oct, 2020. https://www.blueletterbible.org//lang/lexicon/lexicon.cfm?Strongs=G350&t=KJV
5. "Black Lives Matter Is 'a Spiritual Movement,' Says Co-Founder Patrisse Cullors." 2020. Religion News Service. June 15, 2020. https://religionnews.com/2020/06/15/why-black-lives-matter-is-a-spiritual-movement-says-blm-co-founder-patrisse-cullors/.

6. "H6256 - `eth - Strong's Hebrew Lexicon (KJV)." Blue Letter Bible. Accessed 18 Oct, 2020. https://www.blueletterbible.org//lang/lexicon/lexicon.cfm?Strongs=H6256&t=KJV

INDEX

G

J

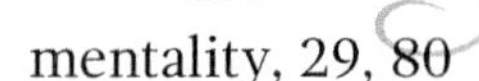

Q

R

Printed in Great Britain
by Amazon